ENVIRONMENTAL CONFLICT

ENVIRONMENTAL CONFLICT

In Search of Common Ground

Jeffrey J. Pompe
and
James R. Rinehart

STATE UNIVERSITY OF NEW YORK PRESS

Published by
State University of New York Press

© 2002 State University of New York

All rights reserved

Printed in the United States of America

Cover art courtesy of Kathleen Pompe.

For information, address State University of New York Press,
90 State Street, Suite 700, Albany, NY 12207

Production by Diane Ganeles
Marketing by Jennifer Giovani

Library of Congress Cataloging-in-Publication Data

Pompe, Jeffrey, 1951–
    Environmental conflict : in search of common ground /
Jeffrey Pompe and James Rinehart.
        p. cm.
    Includes index.
    ISBN 0-7914-5455-X (alk. paper)—ISBN 0-7914-5456-8
(pbk. : alk. paper)
        1. Environmental policy—Economic aspects.
    2. Environmental protection—Economic aspects.
    I. Rinehart, James R.   II. Title.
    GE170.P66 2002
    333.7'2—dc21   2001049806

10   9   8   7   6   5   4   3   2   1

To our spouses, Kathy and Elaine, who not only provided moral and material support, but as artists appreciate the beauty of our environment and the necessity of preserving it.

Contents

Acknowledgments

As any author knows, writing a book is a laborious and sometimes agonizing process that depends heavily on the input of others. We have acknowledged in the appropriate places in our book, through citations and references, those who provided previously published materials. In addition, there are also those who have lent us more personal assistance. We wish to thank Travis Knowles, Bill Laird, and Barry O'Brien for critically examining various portions of our book at different stages of development. An enthusiastic thank you to Matt Bonds who did extensive research and shared insights far beyond the call of duty. Comments from an environmental honors class at Francis Marion University in which Barry O'Brien and Travis Knowles used an earlier draft of this book were very helpful. We would also like to thank the Francis Marion University administration for financial support and providing an environment that encourages reflection, discussion, and scholarship.

We appreciated the expert help of the people at the State University of New York Press, especially Diane Ganeles and Ron Helfrich who helped move the project along. Marian Stokes and Jessica Terrana offered timely help with preparation of the index and text.

Chapter 1

◠◠◠

Introduction:
More than You Know

The enterprise within the social sciences best poised
to bridge the gap to the natural sciences, the one
that most resembles them in style and self-confi-
dence, is economics.

—E. O. Wilson[1]

Imagine a cavernous warehouse with shelves filled
with art of all types—paintings, photographs, sculptures,
and etchings. Now imagine government agents scuttling
down the aisles slashing canvases, smashing sculptures,
and shredding graphic works. Sounds like a scene from a
futuristic story of society gone mad. But instead it's Holland—birthplace to Rembrandt, van Gogh, and Vermeer—
circa 1998. Can we blame such events on the legalization of
marijuana in Holland? Hardly.

With the best of intentions, the Dutch government began
an arts subsidy program in 1949. To assist struggling artists,
the Dutch government agreed to pay a modest stipend to tal-
ented artists in exchange for two or three works of art a year.
The Beeldende Kunstenaars Rageling (BKR), the agency in
charge, purchased the art based on the "needs" of the artist
rather than the merit of the work, and guaranteed payment
regardless of whether the art was valuable or not. With a
strong economy (thanks mostly to North Sea oil revenues)
and strong support from a society that appreciates the arts,
little public criticism surfaced. By 1982, the popular program

1

had expanded to include more than 3,000 artists who were receiving $70 million in annual subsidies.

By 1987, the Dutch government owned 220,000 works of art, most of it sitting in warehouses, and most of it never shown in public or private. Everyone agreed that much of the art was inferior or worse. Good artists didn't want to hand over their "good" art to the government, only to have it sit around in warehouses, and bad artists gladly "sold" their art to the government, the only purchaser willing to buy. A crushed dish rack and a smashed shopping cart are representative of some of the "art." Stories of artists turning in their children's finger paintings or a table top hastily separated from the base and splattered with paint were common.

Beginning in the 1980s, the government began budget-cutting, and the art subsidy was one victim. Although 1,000 artists still receive stipends, the government slashed the program drastically. Despite the cuts in the art subsidy budget, a problem still remained—what to do with warehouses full of art that nobody wanted? Selling the art—even those works that might be marketable—was challenged by the Artists Union, who reasoned correctly that increasing the supply of art would decrease the price of all works of art. In 1994, the BKR permitted artists to retrieve their art free of charge, but predictably less than one-third responded.

A compromise solution is currently being implemented. The government absorbed much of the work in Amsterdam's Artoteek—an art lending library, and slashed, smashed, and shredded the remaining works, to make certain that the works didn't reappear on the market. The director of the collection, Sya van't Vlie plans to use paper shredders on the graphic art, so, "That way we can recycle the paper."[2]

Now, the moral of the story is not that we should recycle, although recycling can be a good thing. The moral is that when you offer someone money and you don't care what they give you in return, you'll get something like graphic "art" suitable only for recycling. Pay more for a certain behavior and you'll get more of it. Also true is that a misunderstanding or lack of understanding of important economic principles can result in poor policy and inferior outcomes.

What is true for the arts is also true for the environment. Subsidize the delivery of "junk" mail as the U.S. Postal Service does, and you'll get trashcans filled with paper heading for recycling centers or trash dumps. Either way, however, resources are being misdirected. We must consider such economic realities to successfully deal with the environmental problems we face. An understanding of simple economic principles would have allowed one to predict the Dutch dilemma and assist in avoiding similar mistakes in other important areas, some environmental.

The Environment and Economics

Few would deny the importance of maintaining some level of environmental quality. The environmental problems society faces are substantial and are of growing concern to Americans and people around the globe. Consider a brief litany of some pressing environmental concerns offered by well-known environmentalist E. O. Wilson: approaching limits of food and water supplies, loss of species diversity, ozone layer depletion, overfished oceans, polluted air and water, global warming, shrinking forests, and spreading deserts.[3] The question is not whether the earth has environmental problems; rather, it is a question of how severe the problems are, what level of environmental quality is desired, and what courses of action should be taken.

Although environmental problems are not new, the environmental movement is a relatively recent development. Numerous voices such as those of Thoreau, Muir, and Leopold expressed important conservationist concerns before the 1960s, but the modern environmental movement coincided with the appearance of books by Rachel Carson (*Silent Spring*, 1962), Paul Ehrlich (*Population Bomb*, 1968), Barry Commoner (*The Closing Circle*, 1971), and the Club of Rome (*Limits to Growth*, 1972). Even the first Earth Day didn't occur until 1970.

The field of environmental economics has evolved along with environmental worries, although many of the economic principles that help us understand environmental choices are not recent. Boulding (1966), Ayre and Kneese (1969), and Daly (1971) were some of the first economists to recognize the interrelationship between economics and the environment. Perhaps the first economist to examine environmental issues was Thomas Malthus, who worried in 1798 that we were running out of cropland to feed the rapidly increasing world population. In his *An Essay on the Principle of Population*, Malthus observed that because population grows at a faster rate than labor productivity, population growth would outstrip food production. Populations would increase until food limits were reached, standards of living would fall, and pestilence and famine would follow. No wonder Carlyle labeled economics the "dismal science." Although right sometimes in the short run, Malthus was wrong over the long haul because he miscalculated the benefits of technological innovation. Neo-Malthusians continue to warn us about population growth and caution that Malthus may yet be correct.

Natural scientists have raised public awareness about the seriousness of environmental problems through numerous well-publicized books and articles. However, environmental issues pose special challenges for scientists because understanding environmental problems and formulating policies to deal with them require an interdisciplinary approach. The hard sciences such as ecology, biology, geology, chemistry, and physics are primarily focused on the laws controlling the natural environment but provide little ground for an analysis of human behavior. On the other hand, social scientists such as economists, sociologists, political scientists, and psychologists study human behavior, but often demonstrate little understanding of the functions of ecological systems. Cooperation between natural scientists and social scientists is necessary if we expect to make the best environmental decisions. Environmental economists are attempting to bridge this gap by examining how economic decisions interact with the environment.

Most scientists in their graduate education programs specialize in a single field or discipline, thereby failing to acquire knowledge in other important fields that may bear on the problem. Psychologists, biologists, geologists, chemists, physicists, sociologists, political scientists, ecologists, economists, and others can legitimately claim a stake in the environmental debate, yet each expert comes to the table with myopic eyes. It is not surprising that so many participants in the debate speak half-truths, are biased in their analysis, and demonstrate unnecessary levels of hostility and rancor in debating the issues. One environmentalist revealed such hostility when he said "economics, and economists are traditional enemies of the environment."[4] This brings us to the purpose of this book.

The authors of this book are economists by training, who are drawn to environmental issues because of personal appreciation for the environment. We have a personal stake, as does most everyone else, in the loss of trees, wetlands, species, wildlife habitat, and in the pollution of land, water, and air. But as we have followed the national discourse over the past three decades, it has become crystal clear to us that first, the debate has been largely devoid of the most rudimentary understanding of simple economic principles, especially in the public arena at the layperson's level; and second, economics has an important role to play in clarifying the issues and in formulating solutions.

We've written this book because we believe that Americans want some level of environmental protection, and want to better understand the nature of the economic forces that affect the environment. We hope to make a positive contribution to the debate by explaining in layperson terms what economics has to offer.

As far as we can tell, the average, well-educated citizen has little comprehension or appreciation of where economics fits into the environmental debate. Yet, we ask these same individuals to vote for congressmen, senators, governors, mayors, local and state legislators, vice presidents, and presidents who craft clean air and water bills, wetland legislation, and multitudes of other environmental measures too numerous to list here. We believe this book will fill some of this void.

In the early 1800s, English economist David Ricardo, in several articles in the public press, changed the way the British viewed the corn laws and changed the way the world looked at international trade. Free trade followed and for at least one hundred years, the British dominated world trade and expanded the Commonwealth to the far corners of the world. As demonstrated by the Ricardo example, understanding basic economics can have powerful, positive effects on the welfare of mankind. We believe a grasp of basic economic concepts can raise the level of discourse regarding environmental issues and thereby improve the effectiveness of environmental policy and the welfare of us all.

Misunderstandings between economists and noneconomists are sometimes the result of the two groups approaching issues from different perspectives. Environmentalists often view actions in strictly moral terms, following imperative standards, which hold that certain acts are right or wrong in and of themselves, regardless of the costs. Barry Commoner contends that "Nature knows best." Carl Pope, associate executive director of the Sierra Club, is quoted as saying "the environment is an ethical issue."[5] Economists on the other hand are more likely to be concerned about end results, comparing options and looking for the best outcome, often from many alternatives. "Society should construct a dam if the benefits are greater than the costs," an economist might reason. Society makes the ultimate decision through elected government officials about how to use resources and may follow either the moral or practical guideline, or take an approach that combines the two. For instance, a compromise approach could be, "We will construct a dam if the benefits are greater than the costs, as long as we do not destroy a species."

While recognizing that we have serious environmental problems, the authors try to consider the issues from a dispassionate and constructive standpoint. In this book, rather than suggest what environmental choices society *should* make, we present some irrefutable economic principles that must be considered in any reasoned approach to solving environmental problems. We examine how and why people make choices, rather than discuss values that society should follow when making choices. We analyze human behavior when confronted with choice, and how humans respond to change. We show how economics can be used to help solve environmental problems, although we also note environmental problems to which economics may not provide adequate solutions.

In order for environmental policy to work, we must understand the economic forces that explain why people damage the environment in the first place. In the final analysis, environmental degradation is essentially an economic problem. Companies choose to dump sulfur dioxide in the atmosphere rather than control it because they make more profit. Developers fill in a wetland because people pay more for a lot to be used as a construction site than for wildlife habitat. Fishers choose to hunt tuna towards extinction because buyers pay high prices and the individual fisher gains nothing by leaving the tuna for someone else to catch.

The Importance of Economics

When human beings must choose between basic items such as food, clothing, and housing on the one hand or protecting the environment on the other, the environment loses almost every time. That is a fact. Some of the most serious environmental problems the world faces are in the poorer nations. The two countries with the most plant and animal species are Brazil and Indonesia. Yet, Brazilians sacrifice rain forest for food production, and Indonesians, reacting to the recent economic crisis, are hunting to extinction species that are found nowhere else in the world.[6] Although the issues are much more complex than this simple presentation, if we had limitless resources, we wouldn't need to make such tough choices.

Even when choices are between less important things, we still incur costs with every choice we make. Trade-offs do exist between environmental products and other products that we need or want. For instance, if we protect an old growth forest, we lose jobs for lumberers. If we fill a wetland for a housing development, we lose valuable wildlife habitat. If we stop the incidental catch of endangered sea turtles by requiring turtle exclusion devices on fishing nets, shrimpers suffer decreased profits and consumers pay higher prices for shrimp. If we impose restrictions on the pollutants that a power plant can emit, we raise the cost of electricity. As a practical matter, we have no alternative but to consider the materialistic side of the environmental issue.

Technology can solve some problems, but we can't expect an engineer to invent a new filter that will eliminate all air pollutants. Biologists can explain why an insect is important to an ecosystem, but can't show society why the insect is more important than a golf course. Lawyers can sue for damages from an oil spill, but they can't stop countless automobiles from spewing noxious fumes. And politicians pass new laws that, even when well-meaning, produce disappointing results because of the machinations of special interest groups. Economics holds the key to resolving many environmental problems because economics focuses primarily on the consequences of choices. To solve environmental problems we must alter the choices we make.

All too often we select easy targets to blame. Business firms are often condemned for the environmental harm they cause. This may be understandable when we see smokestacks belching pollutants into the atmosphere, scarce water being used on golf courses, and tropical forests being cut and burned. As Mark Twain said, "Nothing so needs reforming as other people's habits." However, the problems are more complex and interesting than they first appear, since in addition to businesses, consumers and governments also play major roles.

The Environmental Protection Agency estimates that in 1997 adhering to federal environmental regulation cost the United States $170 billion.[7] If this estimate is correct, the cost of environmental compliance is 2.2% of Gross Domestic Product (GDP).[8] No other country spends as much on environmental protection. As a consequence, we face growing acrimony over the size of the bill and who should pay. Perhaps this is best illustrated by the increasing litigation over the "takings" issue. Law suits are popping up all over the country brought by landowners in attempts to prevent local, state, and federal governments from restricting the use of their lands, thereby reducing value. We believe that unless the various players in the environmental effort arrive at some common understanding of the issues, further efforts to maintain environmental standards will be placed in jeopardy.

There are some positive signs that compromise and cooperation are on the rise. Some ecologists and environmentalists recognize the importance of economics, and some economists agree that we can no longer ignore the ecosystem when making economic decisions. Recent journals such as *Ecological Economics*, *Environmental Ethics*, and *Wild Earth* offer discussions between economists and ecologists on many environmental topics. Communication between economists and ecologists appears to be on the rise, although many still view economists with suspicion.

The influential conservationist Aldo Leopold cast numerous epithets at economists, dismissing them finally by observing that he "never met an economist who knows Draba." (For you economists—draba is "the smallest flower that blows" and one "that does a small job quickly and well."[9]) Such complaints are not new, however. Edmund Burke lamented centuries ago, "The age of chivalry is dead; that of sophisters, economists, and calculators has succeeded." On the other hand, Samuel Pepys concluded that the three finest human beings he knew were Adam Smith, David Ricardo, and Thomas Malthus—all economists. Of course, that was about two centuries ago.

Telling an environmentalist that you're an economist can sometimes create the same response that starting a chainsaw in a stand of ancient redwoods does. Hazel Henderson was once quoted as saying that "economics is a form of brain damage" and according to biologist, Mitch Friedman, "This view has held sway among environmentalists for decades." Friedman goes on to say that biocentrists view "with fear and loathing" pollution credits and other market-based reforms. To an economist, market incentives are as

much a no-brainer as preserving virgin forest is to an environmentalist. To Friedman's credit, however, he thinks that
biocentrists should "pay more attention to economics."
While admitting that he didn't take a single economics
course in college he says, "But just as my failure to study
political science hasn't prevented me from engaging in policy activism, I've been too pragmatic to avoid poking around
the edges of what economics has to offer."[10]

Economists and many noneconomists for that matter
sometimes view environmentalists as misanthropic hyp-
ocrites, driving along in gas-guzzling, exhaust-spewing
sport utility vehicles and sipping espresso made from coffee
beans grown by Brazilian farmers, who in the process of
growing coffee beans destroy ecosystems. Wallace Kaufman,
who has lobbied for environmental groups, notes, "The fact
that most environmentalists quickly return to the comforts
of capitalism after a brief fling with rural life or volunteer
work among the poor does not deter them from continuing
to endorse poverty and the simple life for others and pro-
claiming the joys."[11]

We hope to avoid being either the accuser or accused, but
instead contribute to a bridging across disciplines. We address contentious issues between environmentalists and
economists, but make special efforts to avoid a battle between
"us and them." Many recent books and articles have taken
the confrontational approach. Julian Simon, Dixie Ray Lee,
Ronald Bailey, Paul Ehrlich, David Orr, and Jeremy Rifkin
are a few who have contributed to an adversarial approach.
We avoid antagonistic posturing and instead provide a book
that contributes to more rational and informed choices.

We believe a synthesis of ideas is essential for progress
on environmental issues. We wish to aid the Mitch Fried-
mans and the E. O. Wilsons of this world in their attempt to
glean the economic principles that are essential to an understanding and formulation of solutions to our environmental concerns. We do not believe environmentalists have
a monopoly on caring about the environment. Economists,
too, must live in this world. Economists, too, enjoy uncrowded beaches, wild places, and virgin forests. Econo-

mists have no fight with the biologists, chemists, and physicists about the seriousness of global warming, species extinction, DDT, acid rain, and lost wetlands. Natural scientists must provide the basic data and analysis on the extent of such problems, not economists, but economists have much to offer in formulating policy solutions.

Environmentalists and economists, however, may have their differences. Traditional environmentalists seem to want zero tolerance for altering the environment, while economists ask how clean should the air and water be? Additionally, economists have policy tools in their bag that are often superior to those of environmentalists in dealing with environmental problems.

Just as there are biological systems, geological systems, political systems, and sociological systems, there are economic systems. The environmental practitioner must link these systems in order to understand causes and formulate workable solutions, and the way to do that is through honest and respectful discourse. Just as there are laws in the natural sciences, there are laws in the social sciences. Just as we must weigh the effect of physical laws when considering the severity of an environmental problem and the solutions, we must understand basic economic laws and principles. If beach erosion threatens homes along the shore in the Hamptons, we must consult coastal engineers and geologists to examine the effect of ocean waves and currents on the movement of sand. We must also understand the economic forces that encourage people to build in such dangerous places in the first place, and how incentives may be used to change their behavior.

Walter Williams stressed the importance of recognizing economic laws in a 1985 syndicated column. Williams explained that Congress would be "laughed out of existence" if it passed a law that defied the law of gravity. Say Congress mandated that all aircraft taking off from New Jersey shut off their engines and henceforth proceed to California. Following such a policy, how far would aircraft get toward their destination? Yet, as Williams points out, the government often enacts laws that require the repeal of economic laws such as the laws of supply and demand. From minimum wage laws to price controls on gasoline and apartments, the government assumes that buyers and sellers will not alter how much they are willing to buy and sell when the government regulates price. When they do we usually express shock at the negative consequences; yet, we rarely link the price control with the bad effects, a sure sign that the economic principles involved are not understood.[12]

A perfect illustration is the gas crisis in the 1970s. In 1979, we had long lines of automobiles at gas stations waiting to fill up. Most people thought the gas shortage was due to some sort of conspiracy on the part of gasoline suppliers: most never realized the shortage was the direct effect of government price controls on gasoline. In Western Europe where there were no price controls on gasoline, waiting lines at gas pumps never materialized even though their gasoline suppliers were the same as American suppliers.

Although traditionally economists have not always explicitly acknowledged that society's choices are dependent on the biosphere (all living plants and animals and their interrelationships), most economists today recognize that economic decisions are dependent on and limited by ecological systems. The natural environment provides the raw materials such as trees, ore, oil, and water used to make the products we need and desire. The production process uses the raw materials and returns the residual (pollution) to the environment. Not only are resources limited, but the environment is also often damaged by the residual created by the production process. Too much waste devalues the air, land, and water required for food, clothing, housing, and health. Too much waste damages air, land, and water that provide us amenities such as whitewater rafting and wilderness camping that contribute to a better quality of life. For the highest level of well-being, our economic system must operate in harmony with the environmental system.

Environmental protection is important, if for no other reason than that we depend on the environment for our habitat. No one wants to spend life in a protective rubber suit because of environmental pollution or develop cancer from carcinogens in the water we drink and the air we breath. Economists want to protect the environment but also want to ensure that the flow of useful goods and services is maintained at a high level.

Alas, identifying yourself as an economist to a noneconomist often elicits a groan and the complaint that he or she would have preferred a trip to the dentist for root canal work to the only economics class he or she ever took. Oftentimes, an economics lecturer traumatizes the noneconomist by droning on in "economic speak." No doubt, many feel like Alice who, when confronted with the poem *Jabberwocky* said, "Somehow it seems to fill my head with ideas, only I don't know exactly what they are." Later, on the other side of the looking-glass, Humpty Dumpty provides an interpretation of the seemingly incomprehensible poem. The ideas became much clearer to Alice. Perhaps we can fill the same role as Humpty, for those interested in environmental matters, although we would never play so loose with the rules. Humpty boasts, "When I use a word, it means just what I choose it to mean, neither more nor less."

We promise to avoid economic jargon (not once do we mention technological external diseconomies), graphs (we draw no dreaded cost curve), and charts, that so quickly put noneconomists to sleep. We present economic principles in a simple enough fashion so that they are accessible to the interested individual. We try to demystify economics. After all, much of economics is common sense. Understanding some basic economic principles can be an enlightening experience. We hope you will find our approach stimulating.

E. O. Wilson has commented that if human beings vanished overnight, other species would hardly register the loss, except for the species that would be better off.[13] But six billion *Homo sapiens* now inhabit the planet earth, one billion more than lived here in 1987, and more are on the way. We may not be vanishing for a while. And, for the near term at least, for better or worse, we humans are in charge.

No ecosystem has escaped human impact—from Mt. Everest to Antarctica to the South Pacific Islands. Along with our numbers and our reach, we have a hunger for products that require vast amounts of natural resources and sophisticated technology that causes worldwide changes on an unprecedented scale. Therefore, protecting the environment requires that we understand what motivates humans to destroy it, how choices are made, what the consequences of these choices are, and how choices may be altered to improve the outcomes.

We live in interesting times, but times when we are increasingly concerned about the environment. Joseph Campbell said that Gods are not discovered, they are created. This is also true of economic systems. However, economic systems are not created in a vacuum, but shaped by the events of each generation. For example, a coalition of events created the evolution of European feudalism to an emerging market society.[14] John Maynard Keynes' theory of government action to counteract business cycles evolved from our experience in the 1930s with the Great Depression, and its recent decline in popularity is owed to the negative results produced by the inherent weaknesses in using the government in a more active way. Recent theories advanced by public choice economists such as James Buchanan and Ronald Coase permit us to understand the limits of government policy in dealing with societal problems. Today's economic choices and systems are products of our time. While many countries are experiencing increasing prosperity, they are also dealing with growing environmental concerns.

The "Queen of the Social Sciences" (a more appropriate moniker for economics, we feel) has something to offer to the environmental debate. We must understand some of what economics is about in order to make a difference in the environmental debate. With or without economics, people are interested, are debating, and are acting on important environmental issues. We contend that with a better understanding of economics, we can improve environmental policy.

Chapter 2

∽∽

Unfortunately, the Best Things in Life Aren't Free: How Economists Think

All of life is making choices; to breathe is to choose.

—A. Camus

According to the 1927 song, *The Best Things in Life Are Free*,[1] gleaming stars, sunbeams, and songbirds are wondrous and free. While we agree that stars, sunbeams, and songbirds are wondrous, they certainly aren't free. Air pollution obscures the sky in many of the world's largest cities, such as Los Angeles, Mexico City, and Peking, hides the stars, and distorts the beauty of sunbeams. Eleven percent of the world's bird species are threatened with extinction, and three-fourths of the world's bird populations are declining because of habitat loss, pollutants, and hunting.[2] We can control air pollution and protect wildlife habitat, but not without cost. Smokestack scrubbers, catalytic converters, and debt-for-nature swaps come with a price tag attached.

It's not unusual for an economist to listen to an upbeat tinpan alley tune, like *The Best Things in Life Are Free* and come up with a dismal interpretation. What compels economists to find cautions where others find snappy tunes? Let us introduce you to some of the workings of the economist's mind.

Being an Economist Means Always Having to Say "Sorry, but, what's it gonna cost?"

The story goes that there was a wealthy sheik who wanted to understand more about economics, so he called in his advisors and commanded that they transcribe the world's economic wisdom into a series of books. To ensure a good effort, the sheik added an incentive—if the result was not satisfactory, every advisor's head would be cut off. The advisors labored mightily and came back with an exhaustive ten-volume set of economic wisdom. The sheik, although impressed, said that he didn't have the time to read so many volumes and ordered the advisors to condense the information to a single book, then to a chapter, to a paragraph, and finally to a single phrase. After much effort, the advisors came back and said, "Oh great sheik, TANSTAAFL—There Ain't No Such Thing As A Free Lunch." This satisfied the sheik.

Economists are continually reminding everyone of the TANSTAAFL principle. In order to understand what TANSTAAFL means, consider a riddle. What was responsible for the following events in 1990: the price of dry cleaning a suit rose by $1, the cost of a Ford automobile jumped by $225, and the price of a gallon of gasoline in some cities increased by $.05? Answer—the 1990 Clean Air Act. The legislation required many dry cleaners to buy refrigerated condensers to trap the dry-cleaning solvent perchloroethylene, which is a carcinogen. Automotive manufacturers were required to remove ozone-depleting CFCs (chemical compound chlorofluorocarbons) from air-conditioning systems. Gasoline producers were required to produce oxygenated fuel to reduce automobile air pollution. In each case the standard increased the cost of the product. The lesson is clear: We can protect the ozone layer and have cleaner air, but we must pay for it.

Now, many would contend that $1 more for dry cleaning a suit is a small price to pay for a healthier environment. Maybe so, but having a clean suit now means having $1 less to spend on other things, an especially heavy penalty for those of us with low incomes. TANSTAAFL is not always a pleasant reminder, but an important one. Who can blame people for their dissatisfaction with the economist's message? But economists aren't the cause of the sad news, only the messengers.

Any time someone says that something is free, you should immediately think of the TANSTAAFL principle and wonder who's paying the bill. Reflect on the American health-care system and how it operates, and this point becomes abundantly clear. Most of us have health insurance, Medicare, Medicade, or get care from emergency departments at hospitals, who are required by law to provide it even if you can't pay. The effect of such a pay system is that for each of us any one trip to the doctor or the hospital causes us to incur little or no cost, although in some cases there are small co-payments. As a consequence, we view most of the medical care we get as being free or close to free. Even with a co-payment or a requirement to pay a small percentage of the cost, our insurance agencies pick up 85+% of the bill. We view a $50 doctor's office visit as almost free; therefore, the full price of the visit to the doctor is not taken into account in making the decision as to whether we ought to go to the doctor. The net effect is that we all over-use health care. Consequently, in the United States we presently devote 13% of the dollar value of everything we produce to health care, more than any other country.

Regardless of how numerous, intense, or worthy our wants and desires, the fact is, a country's resources are limited. Consequently, the goods and services made from them are also limited. We are, therefore, caught in a cruel bind of wanting more than there is. In short, scarcity limits our well-being. Although countries have different standards of living, some poor, some rich, and some in between, all countries have less than what they would like.

From the beginning of time, people have used God-given resources to make things that satisfy wants. They use intellect, instincts, and brawn to transform resources into shelter, clothing, food, transportation, and entertainment, and in the process satisfy their wants. People also use their labor and resources to make tools and machines and develop new technologies that enhance their ability to make even more things that satisfy even higher levels of wants.

Because we must choose which wants we will satisfy, it follows that to use scarce resources to satisfy one want is to deny ourselves an alternative use. In other words, the real cost of buying a new car with our limited income is the ocean cruise we can no longer afford. The real cost of going to college is the income one forgoes by not being able to work at a full time job. The cost of protecting lynx habitat in the Rocky Mountains is the lost jobs and pleasure that would be created by a ski resort. A recent visitor to the Appalachian Mountains made the following observation: "I came to vacation in the beautiful Appalachian Mountains. Because of the ugly and environmentally devastating mountain top removed by the coal companies, I won't return."[3] The visitor puts his finger on the problem we face. Do we leave the mountains intact for the enjoyment of those who appreciate it or do we excavate the coal, thereby holding down the price of electricity? Simply put, the real cost of any choice made is the opportunity given up. In fact, it is this principle that the wealthy sheik learned from his advisors. Every choice, by definition, involves the sacrifice of alternatives.

It is very apparent how environmental matters relate to the TANSTAAFL principle. If we cut a forest to build houses or mine coal, the opportunity cost is the forest environment—species diversity, wildlife habitat, recreational opportunities—that we sacrifice. Conversely, if we choose the natural forest environment, we sacrifice the houses we could have built with the lumber and the additional power we could have generated with the coal. We face such trade-offs with every decision we make. Environmental ones are no exception. We drain a swamp to eliminate mosquitoes, but we lose valuable wetlands; we spray insecticides to increase crop yield, but we kill fish with the farm runoff; we decrease sulfur dioxide emissions from utility plants, but we lose jobs for coal miners and suffer high electricity prices. The trade-off list is endless.

Although we must make choices, substitutes are available. For every product and service there is an alternative—some good and some not so good, but alternatives nonetheless. We may have our hearts set on lobster for supper, but at the grocery store $15.00 a pound may nudge us toward chicken at $2.00 a pound, or pork at $3.00 a pound. In the summer most of us like to see green lawns in our front yard, but during dry spells keeping the grass green requires water, and water bills can get expensive. The more expensive it is to keep the grass green, the better brown grass begins to look as a substitute.

How does the substitute concept relate to the environment? Consider electricity generation. Many power companies burn coal to create steam that turns turbines to generate electricity. On the other hand, natural gas, oil, and water are energy substitutes for coal, each having different environmental impacts. Below, we will consider how various government policies, involving such things as taxes, subsidies, and permits, can entice electric-generating companies to prefer one substitute over another and to look for substitutes that are more environmentally friendly.

Paul Ehrlich, an ardent environmentalist, refers to "outdated economists" who believe that there are substitutes for everything.[4] The fact is that substitutes do exist for everything, although they are generally not perfect substitutes. For example, old growth forest (forests that have never been logged) could be cut and replanted, but although the replanted forest provides good alternatives for lumber, the logged forest may be a poor ecological substitute. Old growth trees, such as redwoods and sequoias, can be huge, (hundreds of feet in height and 10 to 30 feet in diameter), and the forest can have trees of diverse ages. Even the death of a huge old tree shapes the ecosystem, clearing a path for the growth of plants as the tree falls. The fallen tree provides food and nutrients for many plants and animals. Because old growth forests in the United States have become so scarce, the value of remaining old growth forest may be very high.

With all the different alternatives available to us in using our natural resources, how should we determine which choices are best? Should we protect more wilderness or build another shopping center? Should we save more wetlands or build another interstate highway? Should we reduce pesticide usage at the expense of reduced crop yields and higher prices? Economists use a guideline known as efficiency that balances the benefits and costs of alternative choices in order to get the most value possible from resources. Efficiency is achieved when it's impossible to improve anyone's welfare without making someone else worse off. Consider a project to build a dam. If the construction of the dam makes many better off because they no longer suffer from periodic flooding, and none are made worse off, then that is an efficient choice. But if people are displaced, or we lose recreational opportunities in excess of the benefits from flood control, then the construction project is not efficient and should not be built. Our pursuit of environmental quality is a constant quest of weighing all the gains *and* losses—not an easy task.

A Long Time Ago, in a Galaxy Far, Far, Away . . . , Individuals Chose Purposely and Predictably— Just as They Do Here and Now

"Birds do it, bees do it, even educated fleas do it." In the clever old standard *"Let's Do It,"* Cole Porter has everything and everybody doing it. He was talking about falling in love, but he could just as well have been talking about making choices. Even people in distant times and places did it. We can imagine Luke Skywalker, the hero of *Star Wars,* gazing out at the twin moons that circled his planet and wishing for a faster landcruiser or a C-3PO unit that could regale him with stories of the rebellion.

We sometimes compile a wish list of what we'd like to have. Besides food, clothing, and housing, our list may include a new computer, a Porsche, and a trip to Hawaii. But because we have limited incomes, we must choose which of these goods and services we want to purchase. Robert Mundell spells it out eloquently as he makes the case for calling economics the science of choice:

> There is an economics of money and trade, of production and consumption, of distribution and development. There is also an economics of welfare, manners, language, industry, music, and art. There is an economics of war and an economics of power. There is even an economics of love.
>
> Economics seems to apply to every nook and cranny of human experience. It is an aspect of all conscious action. Whenever decisions are made, the law of economy is called into play. Whenever alternatives exist, life takes on an economic aspect.[5]

How do people make choices? Since choices must be made, it follows that prudent people would rank wants in terms of relative importance and purchase goods yielding the highest benefit for the dollar spent. In other words, they would try to get the "biggest bang for the buck" from their limited income. For example, if Luke Skywalker could afford only one android, say R2D2 or C-3PO, if the costs were the same, we may safely predict that Luke would choose the one yielding the higher benefit. Conversely, if Luke felt that the two units were of comparable value, but R2D2 was cheaper, Luke would choose R2D2. The bottom line is that individuals always try to improve their situation through their choices.

It is only through such a rationing scheme that people get the greatest welfare from the limited resources available. The reason husbands and wives sometimes argue over how the household budget will be spent is that they have different priorities; that is, they rank wants differently. Similarly, often the reason we are so interested in politics is that some government agency or bureaucrat has the power to rank wants and use our tax dollars to fund their choices—choices that may differ from ours.

Indeed, environmental goods are also ranked along with everything else, and individuals don't always rank things the same way. Some of us place higher values on clean water, open space and old growth forests than others. For example, this is why the German Green Party was founded. It supports candidates for political office who place environmental goods on a higher priority level than other goods. Many environmental organizations, such as the Environmental Defense Fund, value environmental protection highly and expend considerable effort to further their cause.

Individuals also pursue goals and objectives based on their own perceived self-interest. Self-interest may be shaped and transformed in many ways, but it is a fact that, for good or for bad, decisions are made largely in terms of self-interest. This is not to say that individuals are interested in only material things. Individuals want many things, material and nonmaterial. Not only do we want such things as colas, hamburgers, shoes, and houses, but most of us also have intellectual, spiritual, and aesthetic wants. We enjoy an informal conversation with friends, read the Bible, contemplate the beauty of a sunset, and maintain good mental and physical health. Many environmental goods contribute to the latter two categories. Individuals are scrambling to satisfy their own wants, whether material or nonmaterial. And it is to our own peril if we ignore that fact in making decisions about environmental decisions.

As incomes and awareness about environmental goods increase, we would expect that individuals would demand more environmental goods. Consider an example. Dry cleaners use perchloroethylene, or perc, to clean clothes. Perc is toxic, and according to a 1995 Environmental Protection Agency (EPA) report is a "probable human carcinogen." Some dry cleaners have started using more environmentally-friendly dry cleaning chemicals, and marketing to consumers who are concerned about the environment and their health. Also, the "green" cleaning does not have the dry cleaning smell that customers find undesirable. Environmentally conscious consumers are flocking to companies such as "Cleaner by Nature" in Colorado, and wherever available. Admittedly, the "green" cleaners are also profitable because they have been able to keep prices competitive with traditional dry cleaners.[6] The government will probably phase out perc eventually, but private firms are already doing it, because they realize that most people prefer a cleaner environment to a dirtier one—*especially if it doesn't cost more.* And this means more profits for the business firm.

Data from surveys show Americans like a cleaner environment, but they don't always want to pay for it, because they can't also have other things if they pay to have a cleaner environment. Perhaps this is one of the reasons the government mandates certain environmental standards. It is a way of concealing the costs. For instance, auto makers are required to install catalytic converters on all cars sold in the United States. The result is unquestionably cleaner air, but it comes at a higher cost hidden in the overall price of cars. No car buyer can sort out just how much of a car's $25,000 price is due to the catalytic converter.

Decision making is further complicated by the fact that the amount of benefit one gets from an additional unit of something is not constant. For example, Han Solo may get $2 worth of enjoyment from his first banthaburger, but only $1.50 from the second, and $1 from the third. Each additional banthaburger gives him less additional satisfaction because he is a little less hungry. How will Han decide how many banthaburgers to scarf up? Han will buy a banthaburger if the additional benefit is greater than the additional cost. If banthaburgers sell for $1.75 each, Han will buy the first, but not the second or third. Because Han has a limited income (and a lot of debt), he might prefer to buy a soda rather than the second or third banthaburger. Comparing costs and benefits on the last unit is looking at decision making at the margin. This is precisely how individuals weigh alternatives and make choices. Such predictable behavior allows us to *understand* and *anticipate* the choices that people will make. The diminishing benefit that Han receives dictates a negative relationship between price and the number of banthaburgers, because as Han's satisfaction from an additional banthburger declines, his willingness to pay declines, and the price must also decline.

How many times have you been told, "anything worth doing is worth doing well?" As Nobel prize-winning economist James Buchanan has suggested, the response to this statement distinguishes a noneconomist from an economist. As popular as this old adage is, people simply don't act that way—and shouldn't. Individuals, quite rationally, undertake an activity when the additional benefit is greater than the additional cost. So, cleaning the garage is only worth doing if the additional benefit (a neater garage) is greater than the additional cost (giving up a day fishing). And, how clean do you really want the garage to be? Every hour spent cleaning means a cleaner garage, but it's one less hour fishing, and there are smaller and smaller marginal gains in each increment of cleanliness. Recognizing that there is a declining marginal gain associated with everything we acquire tells us a lot about how consumers make decisions, and about how society, through government, should make decisions.

To further illustrate this point, consider another example. We can probably all agree that an education is very important. So most of us are very willing to pay taxes for teachers, school buildings, and supplies. But how much education are we willing to pay for? Should we fund all students through grade 12? Four years of college? Graduate school? Professional schools? Purposeful and rational decision making would require that we examine the net gain from the last year of schooling relative to what could be gained if the money were spent instead on highways, housing for the poor, or cleaning up polluted rivers. In other words, getting an additional unit of education is a very good thing, but not to the exclusion of everything else. There may be some net gain from an additional course, therefore, education is "worth doing," but the question is: Is it "worth doing well," that is, how much do you want or how sophisticated do you want your knowledge to be? The gain from each additional unit of education declines while the cost in forgone opportunities rises.[7]

We also may and must apply the concept of marginal decision making to environmental issues. For example, when a farmer cuts, clears, and plows a field to plant wheat, a forest is sacrificed. Rational decision making requires that at the margin we must measure the welfare gain in wheat output from plowing another acre of forest against any lost benefit associated with that acre of forest that is no longer there. If the welfare gain from the last acre used as a forest is greater than the welfare loss from less wheat output in the interest of efficiency and human well-being, we should protect the forest.

Not only must we recognize that trade-offs exist, but we must also make the trade-off choices at the margin. Consider the benefits and costs associated with something like pollution control. Should we reduce the concentration of contaminants in drinking water to 4 parts per billion, 3 parts, 2 parts? Every incremental change will alter both the cost and benefit amount. It is not prudent or wise to simply favor cleaner water and "hang the cost." If the additional benefit from a specific incremental improvement in water quality is greater than what we must sacrifice to get it, say higher product prices, then we should reduce pollution. As we control more of a particular pollutant, considering trade-offs at the margin will be especially important because reducing additional amounts of pollution generally becomes increasingly expensive.

How to Get What You Want

Another important consideration about human behavior is that it is not constant. Moreover, it is important, indeed imperative, that we understand why and how individuals alter their plans and actions. Incentives produce predictable changes in human behavior. Just as it's true that you get what you pay for, it's also true that incentives create the outcomes you may want. That's why we need to be careful what signal we send with an incentive. As we reported in chapter 1, the Dutch got art that was suitable for recycling but not for hanging in an art museum because they handed out payment regardless of quality.

The former Soviet economy operated under a command system with a central committee that decided what goods and services to produce. When the committee communicated the output targets to the factories, workers still needed some encouragement to meet the goals selected. For example, a few years before the dissolution of the Soviet Union, factories were not producing enough windowpane glass. The central committee told workers that if they produced more tons of glass they would receive bigger bonuses. Workers exceeded tonnage expectations, turning out tons and tons of glass. Unfortunately, it was so thick that you couldn't see through it. Chagrined, but wiser, the committee sent out a new incentive: the size of bonuses would be determined by how many square feet of glass workers produced. The square feet of glass flowed from the factories, but it was so thin it didn't get very far before it shattered. Nobody said the bonus would depend on whether the glass was usable or not. Workers were paid for meeting targets, but not for producing quality products. Incentives matter.

Incentives have been effective in dramatically reducing the population growth rate in China. With the largest population of any country in the world and facing the prospect of mass starvation, in the 1970s China implemented an extensive, and intrusive, set of incentives to slow population growth. Parents who limit themselves to one child receive extra food, larger pensions, better housing, free medical care, and salary bonuses. The children will be given free school tuition and preferential treatment when he or she enters the job market. Between 1977 and 1996 the total fertility rate dropped from 5.7 to 1.8 children per woman.[8]

Society can use incentives to alter human behavior in ways that would benefit all of us. Suppose that we determine that smoke from charcoal grillings is becoming an environmental hazard. How do we encourage people to burn less charcoal? If we impose a tax on charcoal, some users will look for substitutes, such as oven broiling or baking. Similarly, incentives also can move firms to produce in ways more compatible with desired environmental standards. We will deal with environmental incentives at great length in the chapters that follow.

Dial M for Markets for a Superior Way to Organize Economic Activity

What's the greatest invention of the past millennium? Here's a couple of suggestions from the *Wall Street Journal*: in 1420 Henry the Navigator invented navigation technology that allowed European explorers to sail to China and the Americas; Guttenberg invented the printing press around 1450; the factory model was invented in Britain in the 1700s.[9] But how about another choice not on the *Wall Street Journal* list—the free market? The thing is, nobody invented it. The market economy automatically evolved in the medieval cities of Italy and Holland as the consequence of a complex coalition of people, activities, and events. Markets just are. Perhaps that's why they are so misunderstood and underappreciated. But the market is clearly a "marvel," as Friedrich von Hayek described it.

To appreciate the value of the market, Robert Heilbroner asks us to imagine an emerging nation that had previously relied on traditional methods to determine what and how goods and services were produced. The nation develops an interest in markets and hires a consultant to explain how a market might work in their country. The leader of the nation asks, "How do we assign people to their various tasks? How do we decide what things to make? How do we decide how much of each item to make? How do we decide on the methods to use in production? How do we decide how much of the things we make should be allocated to each citizen?" The consultant answers, "The market does it." The country's leader has more questions: "What is this market? Where is it? Who runs it?" The consultant answers again, "Nobody runs it. In fact, in a physical sense it doesn't really exist, but it just describes the way people behave." The consultant is uncerimoniously shown the door.[10]

This hypothetical story is far more descriptive of reality than one might think at first blush. One need look no further than the Russian people and their floundering economy to comprehend how little knowledge, ability, and confidence they have in a market system.

Most countries presently rely on a free market system to organize the production and distribution of goods and services that we need. The market is a place where the uncoordinated actions of buyers and sellers set price and output. The market allocates resources such as labor, tools, and raw materials to the various producers based on consumer preferences, which are expressed in the marketplace by what consumers buy, and producers' cost of producing goods and services desired. You might recognize these dual forces as demand and supply. And the amount of stuff that each individual is able to get is more or less based on how much one earns, which in turn is based on how much one contributes to the economy via one's job or profession.

The market is a complex phenomenon, but relatively simple for any participant. If you want to buy a hamburger at the local drive-in restaurant, in order to make the best decision for yourself, you don't need to know the history of the burger you are purchasing. You don't need to know that a shortage of anchovies is causing livestock producers to shift to soybeans for cattle feed, or that low fuel prices make it cheaper to ship the soybean-fed cattle to the market. And you're not interested in the new wage contract that increases salary benefits to slaughterhouse workers or restaurant employees. The market has already accounted for these facts and multitudes of others. Prices of hamburger ingredients have been rising or falling to indicate increasing or decreasing resource costs. The server hands the hamburger out to you as long as you agree to cover the costs of making it. The market lets you to get on with your life, providing products you demand at prices you're willing to pay.

Producers respond to consumer demands by buying resources and machines, hiring workers, and making what consumers want, all in the hope of making a profit. Consider the education of a novice entrepreneur, Tom, who thinks the world is ready for a fast-food joint specializing in healthy food. He opens up Tom's Tasty Tofu Tidbits providing tofu-burgers, sun-dried tofu chunks, and tofu salads. However, as consumers bypass his restaurant in favor of the traditional fast-food fare, Tom realizes that people are not ready for tofu tidbits. He closes up shop, and heads back to the drawing board still with hopes of making a successful business. Bowing to consumer demand, Tom opens up a traditional drive-in restaurant catering to the customer's desires—burger, fries, and a soft drink. Customers hand over their money, and Tom begins to make a profit.

Tom likes the feeling of making a profit so much that he decides to raise prices to make even more profit. However, before long Tom's customers realize the competition is making similar burgers but at lower prices, and once again they bypass Tom. Tom learns another important market lesson: competition amongst producers keeps prices lower than an owner would like. Tom lowers prices and once again makes a reasonable profit, although not the excessive profit he would prefer.

Tom's education is not complete. To make his workers happy Tom decides to provide paid vacations to Hawaii for his employees. Tom's competition pays a market wage to their employees, but they don't pay to fly employees to Hawaii. Tom must raise prices to cover the high costs of Hawaiian trips for his employees. Customers once again prefer the competition's lower priced chow, and Tom will soon be out of business because he's not able to keep costs down. Tom's lesson: competition amongst producers forces them to choose least-cost methods of production.

The market price is a measure of both the benefit to the consumer and the cost to the producer of the product. We are all aided in our choice-making by prices. The less expensive something is, the more of it we will buy. Falling gas prices in the 1990s encouraged consumers to buy more gas and also bigger vehicles that use more gas. The more expensive they are the less we will buy. When gas prices rise again, consumers will replace sport utility vehicles with more fuel-efficient cars, over a number of years.

Sellers respond in exactly the opposite fashion. The higher the price the more anxious they are to produce, obviously realizing that to do so will mean more profit. However, high profits attract new producers who want to get in on a good thing. As profits at Starbucks increased, the number of coffee shops exploded. Conversely, the lower the price, the less they will produce since profit will suffer. Companies unable to cover costs at the lower product price will go out of business. Falling oil prices in the 1990s idled thousands of oil-drilling rigs as oil investors put their money in other, more lucrative, investments. The reduction of oil production was so severe that it impoverished the entire state of Louisiana.

It is this interplay between buyers and sellers that sets the prices of most goods and services. If there are more buyers than sellers at the prevailing price, the price will rise. Notice how air fares rise in summer when more people are taking vacations. And if there are fewer buyers than sellers, then price will fall. Observe how the price of winter overcoats goes down in summer.

Prices stabilize when buyers want to buy exactly the amount sellers want to sell. This is an equilibrium price. But an equilibrium price is not an equilibrium price forever. Consumer preferences change, incomes rise or fall, and prices of other goods change, causing adjustments in how much of any one product consumers want to buy. For example, when consumers read about beef tainted with "mad cow disease" they switch to substitutes such as chicken and pork, and the price of beef falls because the demand has decreased.

Producers also may alter their output levels in response to changes in their methods of production and the costs of raw materials, capital, and labor. For example, if the price of U.S. beef increases, meat-processing firms will buy lower-priced beef from South America. As buyers and sellers alter the amounts they want to buy and sell, equilibrium prices may change, which in turn causes buyers and sellers to readjust, again, the amounts they want to buy and sell. The market is continually adjusting to changes in factors that affect demand and supply. Understanding these simple market mechanics will help us understand why most environmental problems occur and how we might devise policy solutions using market forces.

We have been explaining two fundamental laws in economics: the law of demand and the law of supply. Simply stated, the law of demand says that when the price of something falls, consumers will buy more of it, and when the price rises they will buy less of it. The law of supply explains that as the price of something rises, producers will produce more and as the price falls they will produce less. If the amount producers supply exceeds the amount that buyers want to buy, a surplus is created and prices fall until the surplus is eliminated since buyers will increase their purchases and sellers will decrease their output in response to the falling price. When the amount sellers want to sell is exactly equal to the amount buyers want to buy, price ceases to fall. If the amount producers supply is less than the amount that buyers want to buy, a shortage is created and price automatically rises until the shortage is gone as buyers decrease their purchases and sellers increase their production in response to the rising price. Again, when the amount that buyers want to buy is equal to the amount sellers want to sell, price will no longer rise. Buyers and sellers are constantly altering their behavior in response to changing price.

Really the laws of supply and demand are just plain common sense, but government representatives sometimes ignore them when formulating public policy. For instance, New York City imposes rent controls on apartments, setting rents below what would be an equilibrium rent or price. Therefore, based on what we have just explained about the laws of demand and supply, renters would want to rent more apartments and space, and landlords would want to supply fewer apartments. Consequently, it is a safe prediction that housing shortages would appear in New York City. And, this is exactly what has been the case in that city for decades. We experienced the exact same thing with government-controlled gasoline prices in the 1970s. The federal government placed price controls on gasoline, setting the price far below what would have been determined by supply and demand. As a result, consumers anxiously bought the cheap gas and suppliers reduced their output. What followed were long lines at gasoline pumps, many gas stations closing early as they ran out of gas. The federal government even printed up rationing stamps as a way of allocating the limited gasoline, but the stamps were never used because Ronald Reagan became president of the United States, and one of the first things he did as president was to eliminate price controls on gasoline. The gasoline shortage crisis was over almost immediately.

To ignore these laws in our attempts to formulate policy in dealing with our environmental problems would be pure folly. Free, voluntary, private choices tend to provide us with better outcomes than government regulation because individuals have a better idea than their government representatives what produces the greatest benefit for them. In a free market, generally, people get what they want at the lowest prices, highest quality, and greatest variety. Producers, working in their own self-interest, produce stuff that consumers want so as to receive the highest profit. Competition among firms keeps costs and prices down, and output and quality up. No wonder that most countries in the world have tilted their economies toward market economies.

Understanding a little about free markets will help us better understand environmental issues, because most nations rely on markets to determine what and how to produce goods and services. Also, market mechanisms can be used to solve environmental problems. Although the market is a superior way of allocating a nation's resources, it is not perfect. Markets don't provide enough of some goods, for example, national defense, beautiful landscapes, uncrowded beaches, and clean air and provide too much of other goods, such as automobile exhaust, noisy trucks, dangerous chemicals, and crowded waterways. Environmental problems are a direct outgrowth of these market imperfections.

For all the good that prices do, they sometimes don't tell us the whole story. When producers try to maximize profits and meet the competition, which means keeping costs as low as possible, some production costs may be shifted to others in society. Costs of controlling noxious smells, loud noises, and chemical contamination are costs that firms will not voluntarily pay. A slaughterhouse may dump waste into the river in order to produce the meat in your hamburger at a lower cost. Therefore, hamburger prices are too low because others in society bear some of the production costs.

Nor can firms always collect payments for all of the benefits they create. If a fishing company is careful not to overfish an area, all they do is leave fish for others to catch, thereby losing any rights to the benefits they created.

It is the existence of such costs and benefits not accounted for in a market economy that provides the basis for government action. The government intervenes in an attempt to protect the environment from the actions of consumers and producers and also intervenes to insure adequate public goods such as national defense and education. We spend a significant portion of this book considering how the government might improve the market's handling of environmental matters.

Summary

Be wary of anyone offering you a "free lunch." Because we have limited resources, we have to make choices. While scarcity forces us to make choices, we do that based on the principles we've discussed in this chapter. However, human behavior is not static. There is no one array of choices for everyone for all time. A different array of choices will result if basic circumstances change. Individual decisions are changing all the time as circumstances change, and circumstances move individuals toward lower cost options and away from higher cost options. Incentives change behavior and can effectively change behavior to protect the environment.

Now you have an idea of how economists look at things. Hopefully, you're beginning to get an idea of what economics is about and what role economics plays in formulating environmental policy. We often find that people have misconceptions about economics, like the man in the well-known parable who was born blind, and asks people who can see to describe the sun. One says, "The sun is like a brass tray." The blind man strikes a brass tray and hears the sound. Later, when he hears a bell he thinks it is the sun. Another person, when asked the same question says, "Sunlight is like that of a candle." The man felt a candle and thought that was the shape of the sun. Later, he felt a big key and thought that was the sun. Many people demonstrate a similar misunderstanding of economics. But this does not have to be so.

Chapter 3

⌒⌒

T'aint What You Do (It's the Way that Cha Do It): Why Do We Spoil the Environment?

> What is common to the greatest number gets the
> least amount of care.
>
> —Aristotle

Chaco Canyon in northwestern New Mexico is a dry, barren desert landscape, with few trees and little water. One would not expect that such an inhospitable environment could support one of the most advanced Native American civilizations in North America. Yet, between A.D. 900 and 1200, the Anasazi, or "the Ancient Ones" as the Navajo refer to them, built an impressive civilization here. At Chaco Canyon National Monument one can see the ruins of this once great civilization that vanished abruptly and mysteriously. The Anasazi built massive, multistory, masonry dwellings with huge beams supporting the roofs and miles of carefully engineered roadways. At its height the Chaco Canyon community consisted of a population of thousands living in a comfortable lifestyle. Perhaps more fascinating than the extensive structures rising from the desert sands are the questions that puzzle archaeologists. Why did the Anasazi choose such a desolate location? Moreover, why did the Anasazi vanish so abruptly from a place where they had invested and achieved so much?

Although scientists know little about the Anasazi, who left no written records, Jared Diamond provides a surprising hypothesis: the Anasazi may have rendered the environment uninhabitable. According to evidence from paleobotanists, when the Anasazi first came to Chaco Canyon, the environment was much more hospitable than it is today. A pinyon-juniper woodland that surrounded the community and a ponderosa-pine forest that was nearby provided resources, such as timber and wildlife, for the community. The Anasazi also created an irrigation system to enhance crop production. Scientists suggest that over time the Anasazi deforested the area, which led to increased soil erosion and water runoff. Without trees nearby for structures and firewood and with diminished water supplies for crop irrigation, the Anasazi abandoned the once lush canyon environment that no longer provided the necessary resources to support a large civilization.

Diamond relates a similar story about Easter Island, where in the 1700s, European explorers were perplexed to find massive stone statues standing, but no indication of how or why they were built. When the Polynesians settled Easter Island around A.D. 400, a forest covered the island. The Polynesians gradually cleared the land to plant gardens and used the logs to build canoes, and to move the huge stones used to construct the statues. By 1500, deforestation led to soil erosion and no wood for canoes, which in turn reduced the Polynesians' ability to catch fish, an important source of protein. This series of events led to societal collapse. Today, Easter Island is covered with grassland, statues have been toppled over, and less than one-third of the former population remains.

Diamond suggests that if we don't change our present course, we may duplicate the results of the people of Chaco Canyon and Easter Island. Reflecting on past human-produced ecodisasters, Diamond laments, "The past has still a Golden Age of ignorance, while the present is an Iron Age of willful blindness. . . . it's beyond understanding to see modern societies repeating the past's suicidal ecological mismanagement..."[1] Why do we continue to despoil the environment? Is Diamond correct? Are we willfully blind? If so, why? If not, why do we spoil the environment?

Why We Spoil the Environment

Is it a failure of "our educational system and also the failure of professional ecologists to communicate their knowledge to the general public" of the true value of natural ecosystems and the natural environment?[2] Experts from various disciplines—biologists, ecologists, anthropologists— document environmental problems. Respected scientists (Ehrlich, Orr, Wilson) publish best sellers discussing environmental issues. Academics from many disciplines fill journals (*Ecological Economics*, *Environmental Ethics*, *Conservation Biology*) with discourse. University professors teach courses and award advanced degrees in environmental science and related fields. International experts in all fields travel to conferences (Rio De Janeiro, Kyoto) to discuss important environmental issues. Political parties are dedicated to environmental issues (Green Party), and television cartoons (Captain Planet) instruct children about environmental villains. Environmental organizations such as the Sierra Club and Greenpeace enthusiastically spread the environmentalist's message. Market-oriented groups such as the Political Economy Research Center promote environmental education by hosting conferences and publishing books and newsletters. A plethora of information is readily available about the importance of the environment and the damage that we are doing to it.

Some blame the capitalist system for environmental damage. According to Wendell Berry, "Competition is destructive to nature and human nature because it is untrue to both."[3] Although the market system is an efficient method of organizing economic activity, as already explained, the market system is not perfect. The market system encourages the efficient production of goods and services that we want. It also encourages technological innovation. But it sometimes does not encourage environmental protection. Interestingly though, evidence shows that damage done to the environment is much worse when the state, rather than the market, allocates resources. Contamination and exhaustion of water resources, urban centers with air pollutants five times the legal levels, untreated human, agricultural, and industrial waste, Chernobyl, and military nuclear waste are all part of the Soviet legacy.[4] The Aral Sea in Russia was the fourth largest inland sea in the world and the most prolific source of fish in Soviet Central Asia in the 1970s. Now it is disappearing because the government diverted the water to irrigate the desert for cotton farming.[5]

Is it our affluence and greedy businesses encouraging consumption that turns us away from ecological pursuits? Economic prosperity allows us to live well—too well many would say. Many would agree with David Orr who complains that the billions spent by businesses manipulate and encourage consumption by offering people "fantasy for reality, junk for quality, convenience for self-reliance, consumption for community, and stuff rather than spirit."[6] Noted economist John Kenneth Galbraith maintains that in order to sustain our growing production, we must continue to create wants.[7] Therefore, we continually want more, use up scarce resources, and ruin more and more of the natural environment. In the process of satisfying those wants we create mounds of discarded packaging and waste.

Developed nations use more resources per capita than less developed nations; however, poorer countries often do more damage to the environment. For example, on average, less developed nations have poorer water quality, less sanitation, and more urban concentration of particulate matter. Poorer nations may create more environmental damage because they work to satisfy basic human needs first, and may not have the resources to invest in environmental protection. One of the authors was recently in Brunei and was astonished at the quantity of garbage, paper, bottles, and containers of every description floating in the capital's harbor. When quizzing a local resident, he was told that people have always thrown their garbage in the rivers, and they still do. In more prosperous nations, environmental standards have improved significantly in recent decades, especially with air and water quality. While affluence and consumption patterns may contribute to environmental degradation, it is not the root cause. Indeed, the affluence provides the wherewithal to improve the environment.

Six billion people presently inhabit the earth, and some experts estimate that the planet may have 10 billion by 2050. Most of the population growth will be in developing countries. Increasing numbers of people use increasing amounts of natural resources in an attempt to maintain and raise standards of living. Our modern technology can create much more environmental damage than the stone axes and spears of our ancestors. The industrialization process is our glory, and our curse. We are able to produce mounting quantities of goods but have difficulty dealing with the waste. The environment can assimilate only so much waste. This is a physical fact. Rising levels of resource use and sophisticated scientific developments generate an alphabet soup of pollutants, such as PCBs and CFCs, which aggravate the problem. While industrialization and population growth may exacerbate environmental problems, still they are not the root cause.

Overusing the Commons

People do not set out with the intention of destroying the environment. We undertake activities to improve our welfare, and as a byproduct we unintentionally damage the environment in the process.

Environmental degradation stems from the predictable manner in which humans respond to incentives. When human beings make decisions, they weigh their personal private gains and losses, not societal gains and losses. Suppose an individual finds a nesting pair of red-cockaded woodpeckers (which are on the endangered species list) in a stand of pines he or she was planning to cut for lumber. Because the government forces the property owner to protect the bird's habitat and pays no compensation to the landowner for the lost timber revenue, we shouldn't be surprised when the nest mysteriously disappears one night. Disappointed, but not surprised. A person would be happy to save red-cockaded woodpeckers if society paid him or her the lost value of timber.[8] The underlying cause of most environmental problems is an incentive mechanism that leads individuals to make private choices that create costs for society.

When a person does not individually bear the full cost of using a resource, others bear part of the cost. Consider the story of the passenger pigeon, a slender blue-backed dove, to understand the "tragedy" that often occurs when one does not bear the full cost of his or her action.

In the early 1800s, the naturalist Audubon wrote of the seemingly endless number of passenger pigeons that roamed the eastern United States. Flocks of passenger pigeons, numbering in the billions, often stretched 240 miles long and a mile wide. The flock could cover over 100 square miles when it roosted at night, and the branches of trees would sag under their weight. Who could have imagined that this was a species doomed to extinction? The pigeons were hunted for sport, fed to pigs, and shipped to fine restaurants, where customers dined on roasted passenger pigeon. The last passenger pigeon died in captivity in 1914.

Consider what an early Nineteenth century hunter might have thought as a huge flock of passenger pigeons flew overhead. "Why not shoot as many as I can? If I don't shoot them, the person over the next hill, or the person from the next town will. Besides, so many pigeons—a few hundred won't be missed." To the individual hunter a pigeon is free, and it belongs to the first person who bags the bird. An individual hunter does not have an incentive to conserve, because the individual does not receive any reward for his or her conservation efforts, nor pay a price associated with the bird's demise. In fact, other hunters benefit from any one hunter's restraint by having more pigeons to shoot. Consequently, a rational hunter may even rush to kill more, because the hunter knows his neighbors will be doing their best to get as many as they can, and the pigeons might never be back again.

The individual hunter receives the benefit from additional kills and the rest of us share the cost. Human beings consider private gains and losses not societal gains and losses when making decisions. Hunters freely use the flock of birds since no one owns them. As long as the supply of a resource is abundant and the demand is not, the cost to society of allowing this kind of open access is not great. However, in the presence of sufficient demand we overuse a resource that is owned in common such as the passenger pigeon, and the "tragedy of the commons," a phrase coined by the ecologist Garret Hardin, occurs. Obviously, if there were a way to control the hunting (tough to do unless you can cage the birds), the passenger pigeon would not be hunted to extinction. After all, we don't worry about chickens becoming extinct. Similarly, the American bison in the wild was hunted to extinction, but cattle were not.

A popular view in many places is that our environmental problems are due to a short run view of the situation. Al Gore sums it up this way: "And even if you own the land, it's hard to compete in the short run against somebody who doesn't care about the long term."[9] The fact is this short-run view prevails only when the resource is not privately owned. When a resource is privately owned, the owner benefits from *not* depleting a resource, and instead, saves some for future generations. If future generations value the resource, resource owners would have an incentive to preserve and promote reproduction. Even in the short run and high prices, no cattle farmer would have an incentive to kill off his entire herd. If he does, he is out of business. On the other hand, if the cattle were common pool resources a person would have every incentive to kill as many as he could. Being common property the cattle would be on a first-come first-served basis, and they would go the way of the buffalo.

When a single person or agent does not own and control a resource, that resource is known as a common pool resource. Schools of fish in the ocean, the American bison roaming the plains, and clean air are examples of common pool resources. All three of the resources have been overused and misused. Your front yard, a farmer's herd of cows, and the fish in a lake on your property are examples of resources that are privately owned and are not used to extinction. People take better care of their own property than property they share with others. As the quotation from Aristotle at the beginning of this chapter indicates, the revelation that people will misuse property owned in common is not a new concept. The misuse of common property is the source of most environmental problems. Understanding this point is absolutely essential in formulating workable solutions.

If certain restraints are imposed, owning a resource in common does not necessarily mean the resource will be mistreated. In Switzerland's Alpine Meadows, herders have shared grazing rights for centuries. The pastures are as productive today as they were centuries ago. A success story! Passenger pigeons and pasturelands in Switzerland are both common pool resources. Why have people misused the one and not the other?

Very simply, the key is to control access to the resource. The problem with the passenger pigeon was that no one limited the number of pigeons that could be hunted. In Torbel, Switzerland, a village association controls access by limiting the number of livestock that can use the communally-owned Alpine meadows. Legal documents dating back to 1224 define the types of land tenure and transfers that regulate the five types of communally owned resources: the alpine grazing meadows, the forests, the "waste" lands, the irrigation system, and the paths and roads connecting privately- and communally-owned properties. Many Swiss Alpine villages have similar arrangements where local villages, corporations, or cooperatives own territory in common that they regulate by communal agreements.[10]

Another example of successful control of access to a common pool resource is the American bison, before the Europeans arrived on the scene. Native Americans hunted buffalo herds for thousands of years without depleting herds because cultural traditions and property rights owned by tribes limited hunting. When non-Native Americans began to hunt, without the restrictions, the resource was quickly hunted to extinction in the wild.[11] There are many successful examples of society using common pool resources in a sustainable way, but only when some authority controls access.

We must differentiate between a resource to which no one controls access (known as *res nullius*) and a resource owned in common, but with restrictions on its use (known as *res communes*). The problem of resource misuse occurs when access is unrestricted, a principle that is illustrated by our use of ocean fisheries. All 17 oceanic fisheries in the world are being overfished. Fishers are not ignorant of the fact that by overfishing they are destroying their livelihood, but they have bills to pay and fishing is what they do well. The fish are "cheap," and if they don't catch the fish, someone else will.

Overuse of a common pool resource is costly to society. Because too many fishers go after too few fish, the cost of fishing is high, and the resultant price of fish is high. Future generations also suffer because less, and in some cases none, of the resource remains. The overuse of a commonly owned resource is not just a recent activity of humankind, as evidenced by the number of species, such as the woolly mastodon, the dodo, Stellar's sea cow, and the quagga, that our ancestors hunted to extinction.[12] We continue to over-hunt species, although today species extinction is more often due to habitat destruction, such as clear-cutting the Amazon rain forest for farming.

Overusing the Commons and Environmental Pollution

We can also use the "tragedy of the commons" to explain environmental pollution. With pollution, we don't take something (like pigeons) out of the commons but instead we put obnoxious stuff (like sulfur dioxide) into the commons. Business firms don't put bad stuff into the commons because they are bad people who enjoy making others worse off. Instead, they want to produce goods at the lowest possible cost, so that they can compete with their competitors in providing the best deal for their customers. As a rule, the lowest cost way of disposing of waste is simply dumping it into the commons, that is into the air or water. Consumers, who like to buy products at the lowest possible price, also benefit from companies dumping untreated waste into the commons. However, because the price charged to the customer does not include the full cost of production, including the cost of disposing of the effluent, society is worse off and in this sense, the market economy is to blame.

Here's an example. In the process of making garbage bags (made out of recyclable plastic), a company dumps an untreated chemical that is harmful to aquatic life into a lake. A fisher who was hoping for a big catch is now a little worse off, as dead fish float to the surface of the lake. The dead fish represent a negative externality, which occurs when someone's actions unintentionally harm a bystander. The company doesn't wish to harm the environment or the fisher, but is simply providing a product (the garbage bags) that consumers want, at the lowest cost to the consumer. Citizens could send signals to business that we want a cleaner environment by buying only "green" products, buying only fuel-efficient cars, and products that don't wear out "too soon," yet many don't.

The overuse of a common pool resource, like a lake, is basically the result of poorly-defined property rights. If someone owned the rights to the lake and fish, the owner could charge the polluter for using the lake as a waste depository. Faced with paying a fee for dumping the pollution in the lake, the company might choose to invest in technology that eliminates the harmful effects of the chemical runoff. Property rights also must be enforceable. If others can abuse your property with impunity, because of the inability to enforce those rights, resources can still be misused.

The problem is more difficult to solve if the pollution is coming from a great distance, and is being dumped by many polluters—like the problem of acid rain. For example, electric utilities in the Midwest burn coal to produce electricity, which creates sulfur dioxide that mixes with other airborne pollutants to create acid rain, which in turn drifts miles away and pollutes southeastern lakes and streams. In this case there are no clearly-defined and enforceable property rights to the air; consequently, the air is common property subject to misuse.

Negative externalities are also ubiquitous. Anyone watching television or using mobile phones contributes to a negative externality. Each year, as many as 5 million birds are killed by television and mobile phone towers.[13] Anyone who drives an automobile contributes to harmful runoff from roadways. Someone who disturbs the quiet of a lake by riding a jet ski or sounds a siren in the middle of the night also creates a negative eternality.

What can we do about overusing common pool resources such as air and water? As we discussed earlier, we must control access—not always an easy task. One way is to use government-imposed restrictions. A second way is to tax the activity or charge a fee. Another way is to privatize the common pool resource, which means allowing individuals to own the resource. For example, some trout streams in Montana are owned privately, and consequently are better preserved than trout streams that have open access. Some resources, however, are more difficult to privatize than others are. For example, fencing the open sea is more difficult than fencing the western open range. The physical nature of the resource is part of the problem. Some say that the only solution is to have the government operate as the gatekeeper, and as the planet becomes more populated, the gatekeeper must become increasingly more active in regulating and controlling.[14]

Public Goods

We have problems with some other natural resources for slightly different reasons. Have you appreciated your local wetland recently? Some people may think a wetland is only good for breeding mosquitoes and science fiction characters, like Swamp Thing. A wetland is much more. Besides mitigating flooding and purifying water, wetlands provide wildlife habitat, open space, and recreational experiences. Quite a valuable resource, and one for which you may not even have to pay. You might say that you get a "free ride" on someone else's provision of the wetland.

An individual benefits from the flood mitigation and water purification even if the person doesn't pay for the wetland. Even if the owner of the wetland wanted to exclude someone who didn't pay, the owner would have a difficult time of it. However, the benefit you receive from the wetland doesn't make others, who also benefit from the wetland, any worse off. When one's use of a resource doesn't detract from another's enjoyment of the resource, and it is difficult to exclude someone who doesn't pay for the resource, the resource is truly a public good.

Sometimes we have a problem with the market provision of public goods. Say that we need to collect $100,000 to preserve a wetland. Would we be able to collect enough contributions from all those who benefit? Probably not, because since the wetland is indivisible, there is a human tendency for some to think they could "ride free," knowing that others will pay. Even if we value wildlife, we may not contribute, figuring that others will. Unfortunately, they won't contribute, at least not enough. Because a private company or individual owner will not be able to collect enough to cover the cost of such a good, they have little interest in providing it. Consequently, the government may be required to guarantee the provision of the desirable amount. How much would the Department of Defense collect if military "taxes" were voluntary? It's not that we don't favor a strong defense, it's just that we expect others to step forward, letting the rest of us "ride free."

The problem with common pool resources and public goods is that the incentives in place don't provide the outcomes we want. Since people react predictably to incentives, can we use incentives to protect the environment? Indubitably. By privatizing common pool resources and using taxes and subsidies we can move people toward better choices that will preserve the commons and provide the proper amount of public goods. Incentives are the cat's meow. This is an area where government involvement, if handled properly, could improve the well-being of society.

We examine specific government policies based on these concepts in the following chapters.

Subsidizing Environmental Damage

Government sometimes causes environmental damage with subsidies. Many vested interest groups lobby politicians and government bureaucrats in support of "good causes" such as economic growth, national security, protecting jobs, and helping the poor. Presidents and Congress often oblige them with financial support through subsidies. Most proponents of subsidies start out with noble intentions. Unfortunately, even the best-laid plans often are costly, inefficient, and damaging to the environment. Subsidies distort market signals, sending the message that the cost is lower than it actually is, so that we overuse and misuse resources.

Consider the case of the Hamptons, where many of the rich and famous have multimillion dollar homes fronting the shore along this exclusive section of Long Island, New York. Some 8,000 waves a day pound the shoreline. Each wave shifts millions of grains of sand and brings disaster closer and closer to the million-dollar properties that line the seashore. Hurricanes and northeasters have battered barrier islands for years. A 1938 hurricane wiped out development along the entire Long Island coast and opened up Shinnecock Inlet. In recent years, as erosion has accelerated because of the groins built to protect the inlet, some 200 homes have been washed away.[15]

Such threats present little concern for most property owners. The Federal Government comes to their rescue by providing funds for beach nourishment, low-cost flood insurance, and repairing or replacing damaged roads, parks, and utilities. The Hamptonians, consequently, bear very little of the costs associated with their living in such a hazardous place. The rational Hamptonian would ask: Why not build elaborate houses close to the sea to enjoy the atmosphere and view since most of the costs are borne by others? They may give little or no thought to the fact that others pay the costs of their actions. However, they are aware that the costs do not fall on them. Unfortunately, the Hamptons is not a unique case. Topsail Island, North Carolina, Folly Beach, South Carolina, Galveston Island, Texas, and many other coastal communities receive the same subsidies.

People continue to move to the shoreline in droves despite the dangers from hurricanes, winds, and tides. We are drawn to the coast by its tranquillity and beauty. As the Hampton story illustrates, our government at federal, state, and local levels has aided us in this transition by reducing the costs to the property owners living there. In 1968, the Federal government passed the National Flood Insurance Act, which provides low-cost insurance for property owners. Machinists in Pennsylvania, farmers in Kansas, and teachers in Kentucky provide tax dollars that are used to subsidize those of us who choose to build in dangerous coastal areas. Between 1978 and 1995, U.S. taxpayers paid almost $2.6 billion for repetitive losses (an insured property that has sustained two or more flood losses of at least $1,000 in any 10-year period).[16] And then there's the Federal Emergency Management Agency (a nefarious group, as all X-Philes are aware) providing assistance during emergency situations. And government subsidies such as these are not confined to coastal areas. Many other property owners build in "harms way" along rivers such as the Mississippi, on high California plateaus subject to mud slides, and on sun-drenched rolling hills that pose high risks of fire, and so on.

The problem with coastal subsidies involves more than an equity issue over who pays the bills. The subsidies encourage people to move into environmentally-sensitive areas, thereby causing irreparable harm to the environment, such as habitat and wetland loss, pollution from runoff, leveled sand dunes, denuded shorelines, and silted streams. If subsidies were not available, less environmental harm would occur because fewer people would choose to live in such fragile areas.

Thomas Sowell sums up the issue:

> The media love to interview disaster victims who say that they are going to go back to the homes that were burned, flooded or otherwise done in. It is supposed to show "courage."
>
> If they did this with their own money that might show courage—or foolhardiness, as the case may be. After all, it is no great secret that houses slide down hills in California during winter rains and burn up during the summer brush fire season. Nor is there any great mystery about hurricanes striking the Gulf Coast or that various other places around the country are subjected to flooding again and again.
>
> When it is subsidized, it is not courage. And when it is somebody else's tax money being handed out, it is not compassion.[17]

Water markets are another area where governments create inefficiencies and wastefulness with subsidies. Water is a resource that we must have to survive, although like other resources, we can make due with less. Although water covers three-fourths of the planet, in arid regions and during periods of drought, we have too little water. Because world-wide water use has tripled since 1950, experts project that shortages will become more widespread.[18] Unfortunately, government policies exacerbate our water scarcity problems.

In the mid-1960s, New York went through a severe period of drought. Since New York City drew its water from lakes in the Catskills northwest of the city and since the lakes were almost dry, the City had to take drastic action to limit water use. Local newspapers ran contests for the best ideas on reducing the water shortage. When economists began to look at the problem, they discovered that most apartments in the city had one water meter and that water was simply included in the rent payment. Viewed from the water user's (that is, the renter) point of view, there was no incentive to conserve water. Reducing water usage does not lower one's rent nor would using more raise one's rent. Such a water subsidy policy clearly exacerbated New York City's water problem and provided no mechanism for remedying the problem.

Often, we misuse water resources because government policies underprice this necessary and scarce resource. Traditionally, water has been treated as a free resource. Water in urban areas usually is provided by a regulated utility, which generally prices water below the cost of provision. Prices are set too low, partly because water is viewed as a necessity. By setting the price too low for households, businesses, and farmers, we send a signal that water is abundant and can be wasted. Therefore, people use more water than is necessary for such things as landscaping, plumbing, and industrial purposes.

Water is both a nonrenewable (aquifers) and renewable (oceans) resource. The overuse of aquifers creates an intergenerational problem. In the United States, groundwater is being withdrawn at four times its replenishment rate. In the Western high plains, farmers are rapidly depleting the Ogallala Aquifer, the world's largest groundwater basin. Many coastal aquifers have been so depleted that seawater is filling the cavities, reducing the quality of the remaining water.

In addition to setting prices too low, the Government subsidizes the costs of operation, maintenance, and capital in water markets. The U.S. farmer pays only one-fifth of the true cost of irrigation from federally-funded water projects.[19] Studies show that most irrigation projects, especially in the Western United States, do not make economic sense. Politicians continue the pork barrel projects because powerful lobbying groups (such as farmers) gain a lot.[20] Because water is provided at such low cost, farmers irrigate more than necessary and don't follow water conservation methods. Often, farmers grow "thirsty" crops such as rice, cotton, and alfalfa that could be grown cheaper elsewhere, except for the subsidy. Also, because the price paid by farmers is often much less than residential users pay, market use is skewed. For example, in Los

Angeles residential users pay $250 per acre foot of water, while farmers pay only $10.

Where prices are set more in line with the true cost of the resource, consumers have decreased water usage significantly. Such was the case in Tucson, Arizona, when the city board voted to increase water prices because of serious water shortages. However, local politicians who supported the measure also paid a price. In a recall election, unhappy residents booted out the city board, although board members had done the right thing.[21]

Also, subsidized water projects create environmental damage from water storage and delivery. The city of Los Angeles diverted so much water from Mono Lake that aquatic and bird life were affected. The government encourages the overuse of resources other than water by subsidizing activities such as logging, mining, energy use, and livestock grazing. Subsidies for use of natural resources add up to $650 billion worldwide.[22] Also, land is not put to its highest and best use when subsidies distort prices. We could improve matters considerably by phasing out subsidies and pricing resources based on their true cost.

Special interest groups often tap the largess of the government, and in so doing impose a heavy cost on the rest of society. They do so by contributing to political campaigns and are repaid through government subsidies. This particular flaw in democratic government is especially costly to the environment. The Iron Triangle is clearly revealed in the behavior of the Bureau of Reclamation, politicians, and large western landowners, who get irrigation water at heavily subsidized prices. The Bureau of Reclamation has resisted efforts to raise water prices as they protect the interest of a few landowners, who make substantial contributions to political campaigns.

Search the whole world over, and it would be difficult to find a subsidy that you'd be proud to call your own. Taxpayers pay and the environment suffers. Yet, no politician ever proposed "let's waste taxpayers' dollars and ruin the environment." Unfortunately, even when motives are admirable, the results are usually not.

Summary

Karl Marx, the philosophical father of socialism, said that resources should be owned in common, to prevent inequitable income distribution. The Marxist adage, "from each according to his ability, to each according to his needs," sums it up very well. As we noted, and as evidence shows, the environment was treated poorly under communism. Common pool resources may also be treated poorly in market systems, unless access is controlled. So "the way that cha do it" needs to take into account that decision makers weigh private benefits and costs and often shift some costs onto society.

The Anasazi and Easter Islanders, because of a lack of access control, perhaps due to environmental ignorance, damaged their environment to the point of total collapse. Other societies, however, have instituted controls on common pool resources with some degree of success, e.g., Switzerland's Alpine Meadows. But, common pool resources may also be protected with clearly-defined property rights. We will spend much of the upcoming chapters discussing ways that we can avoid the same debacle.

Chapter 4

∽∾

Who Will Buy?:
Weighing the Value of Environmental Goods

The art of economics consists in looking not merely at the immediate but at the longer effects of any act or policy; it consists in tracing the consequences of that policy not merely for one group but for all groups.

—Henry Hazlitt, *Economics in One Lesson*

The movie *Butch Cassidy and the Sundance Kid* starts with the outlaw Butch (Paul Newman) casing a bank for a potential robbery. After observing the many new deterrents, including a security guard, Butch asks the guard, "What happened to the old bank? It was beautiful." "People kept robbing it," responds the guard. "A small price to pay for beauty," Butch grumbles. A small price for Butch, who finds beauty in historic buildings (and poorly-defended banks), but a price that bank stockholders and depositors were not willing to pay.

Before we can decide whether we're willing and able to pay the price for something, we need to know how valuable it is. After all, "birds gotta fly, fish gotta swim," and we all gotta weigh the benefits and costs of our actions. According to E. O. Wilson, ". . . close studies by zoologists of the daily schedules, feeding behavior, and energy expenditures of individual animals have revealed that territorial behavior evolves in animal species only when the vital resource is *economically defensible*: the energy saved and increase in survival and

53

reproduction due to territorial defense outweigh the energy expended and the risk of injury and death."[1]

In this chapter we consider some of the nuts and bolts of benefit-cost analysis, a process that may help us make better decisions. We also consider what constitutes value and how to estimate the value of environmental goods, some sold in the marketplace and some not sold in the marketplace. Historically, environmentalists often have disdained any notion of quantifying benefits and costs of environmental protection, feeling that something as vital as the environment couldn't be reduced to dollars and cents. However, recent signs indicate that environmentalists are turning to economists for help in determining the value of environmental resources with the expectation that such valuation will actually promote greater protection of valuable resources. In a recent lawsuit several environmental groups, including Friends of the Earth and Forest Guardians, use a benefit-cost approach to argue that forests actually generate more income when uncut than when logged. As we'll see in this chapter, benefit-cost analysis in addition to providing a sound basis for decision making may well be a friend to the environmental cause.

What is Value?

Over 2000 years ago Publilius Syrus said that, "Everything is worth what its purchaser will pay for it." In other words, the value of something is the maximum amount people are willing to pay for it. If someone willingly pays $8 to enter a national park, he or she must value the experience at least that much; otherwise, he or she wouldn't enter.

Individuals assign values to all kinds of things based on personal preferences, which in turn are fashioned by a multitude of influences from genetic forces to what they read, see, and contemplate. In and of themselves, seashells have no value. They have value only if human beings assign them value. If we derive pleasure in collecting seashells for future viewing or crushing them for aggregate to use in the construction of roads and driveways, in either case, their value stems from the benefit humans receive from their use.

The value of seashells may change over time as human beings find more or fewer ways of using seashells. For example, we may discover that seashells provide an excellent source of calcium, thus boosting their value as a health food supplement. Or technology may create a better-alternative paving material, which would reduce their use for this purpose, thereby lowering their value.

Market price is a measure of such value and provides valuable information about how society should use its scarce resources as we attempt to get the highest level of welfare from their use. The price of a good or service, as determined by the market, is not just an arbitrary number plucked from the air by a price expert. For instance, the price of a salmon or a 2X4 board, which is set by buyers and sellers in the market, reflects the opportunity cost of supplying the item to the market and the value placed on the item by buyers. Indeed, most things are bought and sold in competitive markets, thereby providing a price that allows us to measure the relative value of things.

An important reason for using market price to estimate the worth of something is its common denominator characteristics. Market price is calculated in dollars, and the common denominator characteristic of dollars allows us to measure and compare many nonhomogeneous things. How else could we compare the value of a ton of steel with the value of a plane trip to Las Vegas or a 5-carat diamond with a new automobile. Although market value assessment is not perfect, we shouldn't dismiss its practical benefits in aiding us in making wise choices about how we should use our limited resources. Karl Marx's failure to appreciate market prices led directly to the impoverishment of millions of Russians and Chinese, as they went about setting up their economies devoid of competitive markets.

A caveat about the economic definition of value, which is the definition that we'll be using throughout this chapter, is in order. Although most recognize and accept this anthropocentric approach to define value, others, such as ecologists, may prefer a biocentric approach. For example, Aldo Leopold's conservation ethic considers the integrity of the total ecosystem when estimating the value of a resource. "A thing is right when it tends to preserve the integrity, stability, and beauty of the biotic community. It is wrong when it tends otherwise."[2] Resource valuation and its impact on human welfare would be quite different if we applied the biocentric rather than the anthropocentric approach.

What is the Value of a Soaring Hawk?

Some environmental goods are bought and sold in markets, and we can use their prices to estimate the benefit we receive from them. Other environmental goods, however, are not bought and sold in markets and consequently do not have a market price that we can use to estimate their value. Have you tried to buy any species diversity over the Internet recently? Camping in the wilderness, watching a beautiful sunset, and enjoying the sight and sound of a soaring hawk are examples of valuable experiences that don't come with a price tag attached.

For such nonmarket goods, which have no market price, determining value can be difficult. Without knowing some relative value, we have difficulty deciding whether society would be better off if the wilderness were left alone or cleared for farming; whether the air should be clearer for better views of sunsets or filled with factory smoke as a cheap way of carrying on manufacturing; or whether we should protect the hawk's habitat or construct a new housing development. Yet, the fact is, through private and government decisions, we are making choices every day about the use of these resources, oftentimes with little knowledge about their actual worth, *only their presumed worth*. For this reason alone, it would behoove us to attempt to measure their values.

Even more difficult to quantify is the benefit we may derive from preserving a resource that is not consumed or used in some direct way. Many of us will never visit the

Grand Canyon, but we may value it nonetheless. We call this a nonuse value, and it can take three different forms: option, bequest, or existence value. Option value exists when we would be willing to pay something to preserve the Grand Canyon because we *may* some day get there. Bequest value exists when we protect the Canyon because we would like our descendants to be able to enjoy it. With existence value, we are willing to pay something to preserve the Canyon just to know that it exists, even if we will never actually see it. Many resources, such as blue whales, giant redwoods, and vanishing rain forests, may provide some nonuse value. We can estimate such values, although the methods are imperfect and the estimates are sometimes challenged.

Once again though, we must remind ourselves that there are no free lunches. Because trade-offs abound, we are forced to make decisions every day with some conception of the relative values of things. Unless we have information on the value of our options, the best outcome from our choices is hardly attainable.

Estimating the Value of Nonmarket Goods

Suppose we have a lake that was created by damming a river. Many people enjoy fishing on the lake but pay no fee for the experience. Is the lake of no value to those who enjoy fishing because they pay nothing? Of course not. Suppose there is a proposal to remove the dam, thus recreating the free-flowing river. In the absence of market prices, how do we determine whether we are better off with a fishing lake or a free-flowing river?

We have several ingenious ways to find the value of nonmarket goods, such as our lake. The first method is to simply ask potential users. "How much are you willing to pay for the opportunity to drown a worm in a lake?" "How much would you be willing to pay for free-flowing river?" Such an approach is known as the contingent valuation method and is widely used in spite of obvious weaknesses. A person enjoying a lakeside "worm drowning" or "wilderness experience" may figure that the interrogator wants him or her to pay more for the experience, so he or she might get tricky and say: "Not one penny would I pay to fish on this lake or canoe the river." Clearly, such a response misleads the quizzer and provides misleading information for any decision makers contemplating uses for the property. Consequently, investigators have been forced to become more sophisticated than simply asking for a dollar amount.

In addition to strategic game playing by respondents, other potential problems arise with the contingent valuation approach. Respondents may lack vital information preventing them from making accurate assessments, but answer anyway since it doesn't cost them anything. Or, respondents may not give serious thought in the formulation of their answers since the question is a hypothetical one.

A recent survey result illustrates the problem. The survey was conducted asking half of the respondents how much they would be willing to pay to protect a rare trout species and the other half for actual contributions for their protection. The hypothetical contributions were more than twice as high as actual ones.[3]

Determining the value of wildlife is a difficult kind of valuation question. While contingent valuation is not perfect, nonetheless, we often get useful wildlife estimations with this approach that help with important policy decisions. In a study on the value of preserving spotted owl habitat in the Northwest, economists estimated that each household was willing to pay about $35 per year to be 100% certain of spotted owl preservation. That may not sound like a lot, but when all costs and benefits were measured, the investigators concluded that benefits to society from preserving the habitat were higher than benefits from logging the areas. They also suggested that one way to get everyone on board in support of preservation would be for the gainers to compensate the losers.[4] Such a compensation concept has important potential for environmental preservation.

While efforts to improve estimations derived from the contingent valuation approach continue, it is a widely accepted technique. Indeed, a recent panel of experts, with varied scientific training, was cautiously supportive of the method.[5] And, besides, as Mark Twain said, "It is easy to find fault, if one has that disposition. There was once a man who, not being able to find fault with his coal, complained that there were too many prehistoric toads in it."

There are two other approaches to nonmarket valuation that are commonly used. The hedonic pricing model uses statistical techniques to estimate the value a particular characteristic contributes to the total value of something. For example, if two houses are exactly the same, but one house is located in an area with a wider beach, the price of the house with the wider beach will be higher, thus allowing us to estimate the value of the wider beach. Real estate appraisers routinely use the hedonic approach to determine the value of such things as lot size, trees, garages, basements, and square footage. Using comparables in real estate is another way of producing results similar to those attained with the hedonic model.

The third approach to nonmarket valuation is the travel cost method, which permits us to estimate the value of a nonmarket good based on the cost of traveling to a site. Each year, millions of us visit national parks, buying gas for the trip, paying motel costs, and shelling out entrance fees. The farther one travels the higher the cost and the higher one must value the experience; otherwise, the trip would not be made. After adjusting for other factors such as income, age, and education that might also affect one's decision, we can estimate the recreational value of an excursion in a national park.

In addition to these three commonly used approaches, we have other ways of estimating the value of environmental goods. Sometimes we can use the value of something for which we have a market price as a proxy for a nonmarket good. For example, the recreation experience from hunting is often difficult to measure. However, some hunters join hunt clubs or pay fees to hunt, which may give us a measure of the value they derive from hunting. To further illustrate, consider using the medical costs saved from fewer respiratory illnesses to estimate the value of air pollution control. Researchers used a variation of this method to estimate the medical cost imposed on all of us from smokers inhaling cigarette smoke. Or consider the water purification benefits of a watershed area. One study suggests that an investment of $660 million in development rights would protect the Catskills watershed and would allow New York City to avoid the $4 billion cost of building and operating new water purification plants over the next decade.[6]

Perhaps the most difficult and controversial valuation task is determining the value of a human life. Because societal resources are limited, we are often called upon to make decisions that place a value on life. If a decrease in air pollution allows an individual to live for another year, what is the added year worth, and how much would one be willing to pay for pollution control? Can we put a value on life and consequently place a value on that year? Someone once said, "Life is precious but not priceless." Some question this entire exercise, arguing that the approach is fruitless and unnecessary. The truth is, though, we reduce life expectancy all the time through the choices we make.

Railroad accidents, usually caused by human error, could be avoided and lives saved by using sophisticated satellite technology. But the equipment is expensive—hundreds of millions of dollars. If we spend millions of dollars on satellite technology, we have millions less to spend on other important projects, such as education, a cure for arthritis, cleaner air, or safer airplanes. The satellite technology may also allow railroads to run more efficiently, which would be an added benefit. Still, to invest in the equipment, by definition, forces us to forgo other lifesaving projects. So, to save lives by spending on safer railroad equipment is to lose lives by not having as much to spend on health care. As we saw in Chapter 2, resource scarcity is what dictates the necessity of choice. Which choice should we make? Measuring the value of lives saved in opposing uses aids us in making the best decisions.

Several methods have been used to derive the value of a statistical life. Since people demonstrate a willingness to accept risk in many occupations in exchange for higher wages, we are able to estimate the value they place on their lives. Generally, the higher the risk associated with a particular job, the higher the pay. Since these job choices are voluntary, they serve as a good guide as to how much value one might put on his or her life. Performing as a stunt person in movies is surely riskier than working in an office, but many do it, and the higher pay is part of the reward and to some degree a measure of the value of a life. The difference between wages for a high-risk job and a low-risk job is the value the low-risk person places on his or her life.

Individuals don't place the same values on their lives. Some are risk adverse; hence, it would take a considerable wage premium, perhaps millions of dollars, in order to get them to incur the risk. Conversely, others are less risk sensitive; consequently, less pay would induce them to take the risk and hence endanger their lives. Using income data for various jobs and relative job-related risks, some have estimated that the value of a "statistical" life ranges from $500,000 to $7 million.

Prudent decision making involves weighing the values of the competing uses of scarce resources, which often entails placing value on human life. Does anyone remember the Tucker automobile? This was a car built to very high safety standards, but it was heavy and costly to buy and operate. It didn't sell in the marketplace. Evidently, potential buyers placed a higher value on their money for other purchases than for more safety. Most of us know that larger automobiles are safer than compact ones, yet many of us buy the smaller, cheaper ones for the sake of styling characteristics and gas and operating economies. Automobiles can be built to higher safety standards, but at higher costs and higher consumer prices, which means less is available to spend on safer roads, improved medical care, and many other valuable improvements.

Medical experts say that diet and the lack of exercise are the principle causes of heart disease and cancer, yet many resist altering diets and lifestyle for the sake of better health and a longer life. Clearly we are voluntarily trading years of living for the "enjoyment" associated with our current eating and exercise habits. For most of us life is not priceless. Every conscious decision is a trade-off.

Benefit-Cost Analysis

Sometimes a choice is obvious. "If you build it they will come." Trust a voice from above. "Follow the yellow brick road." So many Munchkins and a good witch can't be wrong.

Outside of the movies we usually have tougher decisions, but we can use benefit-cost analysis to guide us to better decisions. By comparing advantages (benefits) to disadvantages (costs) of a particular policy, we establish a basis and consistent method for decision making. Also, we can determine whether any other projects would provide the same results at less cost, or more benefit at the same cost.

Anything that improves human well-being is a benefit, while anything that reduces human well-being is a cost. If a beach nourishment project adds $1 million worth of benefits in the form of improved storm protection and recreational use, should we do it? Sounds worthwhile, but you would like to know how much the project might cost. If the cost were less than $1 million, you would definitely consider going ahead with the project. No surprises there, but the calculation process is often difficult and involved, but where we are able to make the calculations, we ought to use them in some manner. Let's examine the process of using benefit-cost analysis a little further.

Consider the lawsuit sponsored by environmental groups that contends that forests generate more income when uncut than when logged.[7] Although a forest can provide multiple uses, some uses may negatively impact other uses. If we log a forest we might lose recreational benefits for hunters, fishers, and hikers. The question is, are we better off cutting the trees for the lumber or leaving them for their recreational value? Nonmarket values, like lost recreational benefits, could be calculated by using the methods discussed earlier. We could also include nonuse values such as existence, bequest, and option value.

Additionally, we lose benefits such as habitat for plants and animals, watershed protection, and carbon cleansing activity of forests and incur environmental damage such as soil erosion and downstream siltation. If the forest is old growth, the loss of value from logging could be even higher because a basic economic principle tells us that when something has little in the way of substitutes it is very valuable. Finally, we would add together the cost of logging each year into the future, because the benefits of the forest are lost this year, next year, and for years into the future.

The benefit of logging would be the net dollar value of the timber, and the benefits lost to logging could be calculated and compared with the benefits generated by logging. It is in this manner that computing relative values of alternative resource use can guide us in decision making.

To complete an accurate benefit-cost analysis requires experts in many disciplines. For example, the degree of loss of wildlife and soil erosion and siltation attributed to logging must be measured by biologists and other specialists. Economists can measure the value of lumber and the costs of erosion. While dredging sand onto a beach provides benefits for beach users, it might destroy shellfish beds. Economists can measure the benefits going to beach users, but we must depend on marine biologists to determine the extent of the environmental damage associated with the damaged shellfish beds. Economists may be able to estimate the benefits accruing to farmers or consumers from the use of insecticides, but we need chemists and biologists to tell us about the environmental costs from polluted air and water.

Although computing the benefits and costs is no easy task, we must consider the alternative. Even if we have no estimate for the value of a wilderness, we still must make choices, and some assumed value is used, whether we are conscious of it or not. A better understanding of the tradeoffs would improve our decision making.

Surveys show that 40% of the American public favors a dam project that creates a recreational lake, even if it means the extinction of a fish species.[8] Comparing the cost to society of a lost fish species versus the benefits derived from electricity, flood control, and recreational gains from the dam can be an instructive process. We agree with Kellert when he cautions, "If all wildlife values fail to be systematically assessed and measured, policymaking will almost inevitably be weighted toward commodity production and marketplace objectives. A more rational approach suggests that all values of living diversity should be scientifically and equitably considered . . ."[9]

There are numerous examples of benefit-cost analysis leading to preservation of natural areas. For example, in the 1970s the government considered building a dam at Hells Canyon, a unique wilderness area on the Snake River in Idaho. A study of the benefits and costs showed that the preservation value was greater than the value of electricity and recreation benefits created by a reservoir. Consequently, Hell's Canyon was preserved.[10]

Special interest groups, who expect to gain or lose based on the outcome, will attempt to push policies to promote their interest regardless of the overall benefit or cost to society. All too often legislation is enacted that lavishes benefits on small, politically sophisticated groups at the expense of the majority of the public. We discuss in chapter 7, a benefit-cost study that concluded that the Tellico Dam should not be completed, but the study was ignored. Without the type of analysis provided by benefit-cost procedures, special interest groups will be able to win more often.

The marketplace oftentimes encourages protection of natural areas, obviating the necessity of the government having to take action, which is a real advantage given the inherent weaknesses in government action. We discuss these cases in some detail in the next chapter.

Another use of the methods described in this chapter to measure economic value is in estimating the liability of environmental polluters in lawsuits and other cases. The 1989 *Valdez* oil spill in Alaska caused significant environmental damage to the sea and land. Exxon accepted liability for the damage, which included the cost of cleanup and compensation for the environmental damage. A complete estimation of damage included market use value (fish), nonmarket use value (recreational value), as well as nonuse value (option, bequest).

Using economic analysis to estimate the amount of damage created by polluters is beneficial on several counts. First, injured parties can be fairly compensated. Second, business firms are forced to internalize the environmental costs of their actions. That is, higher costs lead to higher prices with the consequence that consumers buy less of the product, causing producers to produce less, thereby reducing the level of environmental damage. Third, firms will be encouraged to undertake efforts to reduce the possibility of future spills and future liabilities.

Every day in courtrooms across this country judges and juries use calculations made by economists to assess economic loss of life and property for the purpose of compensating injured parties. It is absolutely essential that we extend this analysis to environmental losses.

Summary

Market price reflects the relative importance we place on goods and services. In many cases we are able to use such prices to measure the benefits of environmental goods. With various techniques, we can even estimate the value of environmental goods that do not have a market price. Such information aids us in making better decisions (albeit not perfect ones) about how we should use our scarce environmental resources.

Every environmental choice produces some perceived benefit and some cost. For example, the Endangered Species Act gives us the benefit of biodiversity by protecting the forest which is often the home of the protected species. Yet, biodiversity is achieved at the expense of a loss of lumber. Measuring the benefits and costs would give us some guide leading to improved decision making regarding the best use of our forests. The same can be said for government laws that protect air, water, land, and environmental resources in general.

No one thinks that current techniques used to measure benefits and costs are perfect. But we make environmental choices every day, and either there is some assumed value attached to benefits and costs, or they are simply ignored. Ignoring the benefits and costs doesn't mean that they aren't there. Often, special interests, who stand to gain or lose, expend great effort in influencing the outcome, usually to the detriment of society at large.

We propose that every effort be made to estimate benefits and costs where environmental decisions are made. If we have a high level of confidence in the estimations, use them in reaching decisions. If the confidence level is low, use your best judgment. After all, all decision making has some degree of error risk.

Chapter 5

Lovely to Look At, Delightful to Know: Preserving Our Natural Resources

> There is nevertheless, a certain respect and a general duty of humanity that ties us, not only to beasts that have life and sense, but even to trees and plants.
>
> —M. de Montaigne, *Of Cruelty*, ch. xi

Prognostication is a dangerous occupation. The respected Yale economist, Irving Fisher, assured investors that stock prices had reached a "permanently high plateau,"—shortly before the stock market crashed in October 1929. Interestingly, years before, Mark Twain, who was not noted for his economic expertise, advised that October was one of the peculiarly dangerous months to speculate in the stock market. The others were July, January, September, April, November, May, March, June, August, February, and December. More recently, in 1985 Ravi Batra wrote a best seller predicting the great depression of 1990. Never happened. Only those who followed Batra's investment advice were depressed.

Forecasting impending natural resource depletion has also been a popular, but inaccurate, pastime. One often-cited study is the 1972 Club of Rome, *Limits to Growth*. The research team predicted that copper, gold, lead, natural gas, petroleum, silver, tin, and zinc would be depleted before 1998. Despite the use of sophisticated (for 1972) computer simulations, the Club of Rome's predictions of resource depletion were *as* wrong as Truman's "defeat" at the hands of Dewey.

67

Incorrect forecasts of imminent resource depletion are not new. In 1798, the father of doomsayers, Thomas Malthus, predicted continual food shortages because populations would grow faster than food supplies. In 1865, Stanley Jevons, a respected economist, predicted that Great Britain would soon run out of coal, and factories would be forced to shut down. The U.S. Secretary of Interior, Carl Schung predicted in 1877 that there would be a timber famine in 20 years. In 1926, the Federal Oil Conservation Board said the supply of oil would last only seven more years. Wrong, wrong, wrong, and wrong. Let's examine why predictions of resource collapse are incorrect. The key is to understand how market forces mitigate, rather than cause, resource depletion.

Market Forces and Resource Scarcity

Natural resources can be classified as renewable (fish, trees, fresh surface water, solar energy, and sea bed nodules) or nonrenewable (oil, coal, copper, and gas hydrate crystals). Renewable resources, which regenerate by natural processes (often quickly) will last forever if we use them wisely. On the other hand, nonrenewable resources are more or less fixed in amount because of the millions of years required for creation. As we use more nonrenewable resources today, such as natural gas and petroleum, less will be available for future generations. However, given the proper incentives, people will preserve resources, both renewable and nonrenewable, for future generations.

Societies must decide what to produce, how to produce it, and how to distribute it. Additionally, for resources we must decide when to use them. For a given pool of oil, should we save all of it, none of it, or some of it? Let's consider how market signals might provide an answer to this question.

Resources are valuable not only when they are used, but also when they are preserved. Suppose you own a pool of oil. You could pump it as rapidly as you can, save it all for the future, or pump some now and some in the future. If you pump it all today, you can put the money you earn into CDs or some other investment. But if you expect that people will pay more for the oil next year, you may choose to save some, since you may be able to make more money when the price is higher—a capital gain. How much higher would price have to be in period two to encourage you to hold onto the oil in period one? If you could receive a 10% return on assets of similar risk in period one, and if the higher price provides you with a present value return higher than 10%, you would be better off holding onto the oil for future use. Decisions about how to use renewable resources such as trees and animals would be made similarly.

As we have explained, when property rights are secure, owners have a reason to save some oil, animals, or trees for future generations. If property rights are not secure, however, and you thought someone was going to take your oil field away tomorrow, you would pump as much as you could today. Uncertainty about the future encourages an owner to drain the well dry while there's still time. In fact, this is precisely why the whale population has been depleted. No one has exclusive property rights to whales. Consequently, you gain nothing by conserving whales, for you only leave them for others to harvest.

Forecasters who predict resource depletion often ignore or underestimate the power of markets. For example, some forecasters use a current reserve index to estimate how long a resource would last. The current reserve index divides the current known reserve of a resource by the amount currently used each period. So, if we know of 445 billion barrels of oil, and we are currently using 15 billion barrels per year, the index indicates that we will run out of oil in about 30 years. Some studies, like the *Limits to Growth,* further assume that demand will increase each year, thus depleting resources even faster. But what they fail to see is that if markets are allowed to do their usual duty, that is, prices rise as depletion occurs, resources will last much longer.

Market prices provide valuable information to market participants and create predictable actions. When we use a nonrenewable resource, because we value the remaining amount, the price rises. According to the law of demand, when the price of a resource increases, we buy less. In the early 1970s, when the Organization of Petroleum Exporting Countries (OPEC) jacked up oil prices, people conserved gasoline by switching to smaller vehicles, car-pooling, and reducing travel. Such alternatives were previously undesirable but became more attractive as fuel costs rose higher and higher. Producers also altered their behavior by using energy more efficiently and by looking for alternative energy sources.

Higher prices intensify the development of alternative fuels such as biomass and solar and encourage us to look for substitutes. In the mid-1800s the British were wringing their hands over the rising price of whale oil, the key energy source for lighting homes and streets, and the impending lack of the fuel. The price of whale oil rise from $0.43 per gallon in 1823 to $2.55 per gallon by 1866 due to the over-harvesting of whales. Petroleum was first extracted in 1859, and the rest is history.

Additionally, higher resource prices encourage increased exploration and the discovery of new deposits. In the 1970s as the price of oil rose, producers brought on line new fields of oil in Alaska, Mexico, and the North Sea. There is a limit to the number of new oil fields, of course. Some day, when most of the oil has been pumped out, the cost of extracting the final barrels will be extremely high. At some point the cost may be so high that oil producers will not find it profitable to pump out the last barrels. In a sense we will likely never run out of oil.

Moreover, high resource prices make it more profitable for firms to seek new technology that uses a resource more efficiently. The pelletization process extended the availability of iron ore in the Mesabi Range in northern Minnesota. Similarly, improvements in refining copper increased the supply of copper and the "green revolution" increased food yields dramatically. Higher oil prices in the 1970s provided the catalyst that led to the technology that made cars, refrigerators, air conditioners, and many other products more fuel-efficient.

Finally, higher resource prices lead directly to more recycling efforts. Although the percentage of recycled trash is less in the United States than in many other industrialized countries, today the United States recycles 27% of solid waste compared to 6.7% in 1960. Because recycling has become such a popular pastime in the United States, and because the issues can be complicated, we consider recycling further in the next section.

Mobro's Two Months of Fame

Ever had photographer's cheesecake? Mid-Nineteenth century photographers concocted the recipe. A photographic process from the Nineteenth century, callotype prints used egg whites, but not egg yolks. Because resourceful, thrifty photographers didn't want to throw useful items away, the egg yolks were "recycled" into photographers' cheesecake (recipe in Endnotes[1]). Of course, humans have a long history of recycling. Archaeological records indicate that early humans reshaped broken metal tools into new ones and recarved broken pendants of exotic stones into smaller ones.

Market forces encourage people to be thrifty with scarce resources. As someone once said, "I recycled before it became trendy. They used to call it being cheap." As we mine more of a virgin ore, the mineral becomes scarcer, the price rises, and because we're "cheap" we recycle more. Many of us also feel better because we're "helping" the environment. Recognizing that a plastic bottle thrown into the ocean takes 450 years to biodegrade, is it any wonder that the idea of recycling has become so popular? And of course there's Mobro.

In March 1987, Mobro, a barge loaded with 3,186 tons of New York City trash, left Islip, New York, for what became a fateful journey. What was meant to be a short trip to haul trash to an inexpensive southern dump turned into a two-month odyssey. The novice hauler, who set up the deal, hoped to profit from regional differences in dumping charges, called tipping fees. Unfortunately for the hauler, he failed to nail down a contract before leaving New York, and at Morehead City, North Carolina, the first stop, state officials raised questions about the contents on board. Nervous officials, not sure of what might be on board, ordered the barge back to sea, without investigating. The media picked up on the story, and for the next two months, as Mobro steamed from one place to another (including Louisiana, Mexico, and the Bahamas), the American public got nightly updates on the plight of the Mobro. Eventually Mobro returned to New York where the garbage was incinerated in Brooklyn.[2]

As the barge steamed the seas, with the trash getting riper all the time, Americans recognized garbage as a new menace. Most Americans interpreted the Mobro spectacle to mean that we must be inundated with trash with nowhere to dump it. In fact, space was plentiful, but once the Mobro was branded a pariah, no dump wanted to accept the trash and the public ridicule that would surely follow. The result was a new campaign, inspired by the nightly news and appealing to our moral sense. The new battle cry: reduce, reuse, and recycle.

No doubt about it—recycling can be a good thing. By not dumping newspapers, telephone books, and soft drink cans into the dump, we use less trees and aluminum, and also reduce the trash hauled to landfills, which means that we don't need as many new dumps. So why don't we recycle more? We have an easy culprit to blame for society dumping too much trash—incorrect market signals.

Rather than collect a pile of statistics and charts about how much should be recycled, let's accept for the moment that the supply of waste is higher than we would like. Let's ask why, and then consider what should be done about it.

Most households pay a monthly fee (set by local government) for solid-waste disposal regardless of how much waste they produce. The household that recycles all possible materials and produces fewer bags of trash to be hauled away to the dump pays the same fee as a neighbor who creates mountains of trash, and recycles nothing. The message from the city trash service is "dump as much as you want, landfill space is no problem." That's not true, of course, but that might be how the trashmaker would think of it. Consequently, households throw away too much garbage and recycle too little since solid-waste disposal is underpriced. The cost of dumping is less for the individual than for society. Taxpayers pick up the tab for what the individual doesn't pay.

We have an easy solution for this problem. We can encourage people to pay more attention to the amount of trash they create by changing the message to households. "Because landfill space is scarce, although not necessarily in short supply, the more trash you create the more you will pay. If you create more trash than your neighbor, you will pay more than your neighbor." Many people will reconsider their trash disposal policy. Because people have better ways to spend money, they will likely try to *reduce, recycle, and reuse* more than they did before.

Some municipalities have already altered the policies of trash pickup so that the fees more accurately reflect the cost of taking solid waste to the landfill. In these cases when people dump more bags of trash, they pay more. A study of one such program in Charlottesville, Virginia, a university town of 40,000, indicated that the fee per bag does not have to be high in order to get people to change their trash disposal habits.

The city of Charlottesville began charging $0.80 per 32-gallon bag, rather than continue with a set fee regardless of the amount of trash produced. Waste volume decreased by 37%, and total weight dropped by 14%. (Hmmm. What effect do you suppose this policy change had on the demand for trash compactors in Charlottesville?) What happened to the 1,500 tons per year that no longer ended up at the dump? One-third of the reduction was from households using less packaging and doing more composting (*reduce and reuse*). One-third was due to increased voluntary recycling (*recycle*). And the other one-third reduction—well, no laws of physics were violated, just civic laws—illegal dumping increased.[3]

So, the good news is that a fee-per-bag program will encourage recycling and reduce the amount of waste sent to the dump. The bad news, in addition to increased illegal dumping, is that the program was costly. In fact, because of the high administration costs (almost $0.20) per bag, the benefits to the community were actually less than the costs.

Other government policies, such as bulk postage rates for catalogs and other "junk mail," encourage the production of too much waste. As a result, the supply of trash is too high. Government policies, such as depletion allowances for mining companies, decrease the cost of mineral extraction and thereby lower the demand for recycled materials. Also, because the federal rate on transporting scrap metal by rail is greater than the rate on virgin materials, the supply of recycled materials is less than it otherwise would be.

Valuable as recycling is, it would be unwise to recycle everything. Recycling has a cost, and it is not pollution-free. Recycling involves many processes—collection, transportation, cleaning, manufacturing, storage, transport again, and sale. Each process uses energy and pollutes just as manufacturing from virgin materials does. We create waste like chemical sludge from deinking used newsprint. We pollute the air with sulfur dioxide as we generate the additional power needed to run the machines that transport and process the recycled materials. Recycling also takes time in separating, collecting, and hauling recyclables. Recycling may even contribute to global warming because of the energy use involved.

Americans create about 200 million tons of municipal solid waste each year, which is about three-quarters of a ton per person, and the per capita rate is rising at almost 2% per year. Compare the percentage of waste recycled in the United States (27% in 1998) to the percentage recycled in other developed nations, and people in the United States appear to be profligate. Japan recycles 50% of their waste. However, factors in addition to attitude and character may explain the difference in recycling rates.

Many nations exclude some things from their official measure of solid waste that the United States includes.

When the definition is adjusted, U.S. waste production is similar to most other nations. Also, the United States has more landfill space than most other developed nations. To place all of the solid waste generated by this country in a year in a landfill would require no more than .00001% of the continental United States. If all the waste produced in the United States for a year were put in one landfill, the space requirement would not exceed a landfill 100 yards deep and two-thirds a square mile on each side. We have sufficient space for landfills, but a problem often results from the not-in-my-backyard syndrome, which creates a problem for communities with very little nearby space available for landfills. In fact, total landfill space has actually increased, but so have dumping fees as stricter environmental standards have increased costs.

Although recycling can be a good thing, the question is what and how much should we recycle? In principle, we should recycle as long as the additional benefit of recycling a glass bottle, for instance, is greater than the benefit of simply dumping the glass bottle in a landfill. Since benefits and costs vary from product to product, we must examine each item in order to determine the recycling merits. For example, aluminum is profitably recycled in large quantities because the product is lightweight, easily handled, and production technologies make recycling economical.

Not Enough Fish in the Sea

Market forces often encourage resource preservation, but not always. While market forces can lessen the problem of resource scarcity, both nonrenewable and renewable resources can be misused. Water markets, discussed in chapter 3, provide an instructive example. Because the government often sets water prices too low and subsidizes water projects, water is wasted.

The world's fishery resources, an important source of protein, are prime examples of renewable resources that are misused. Fisheries could be harvested today and still provide fish for future generations. If a fish population of 20 tons grew by a mass of one ton every year, we could harvest one ton every year and still have 20 tons available indefinitely. However, because no one effectively controls access to many fisheries, the fishery is overused, and we have the tragedy of the commons. Many fish populations have been overharvested to the point where the fishery is no longer sustainable. Thirteen of the 17 major ocean fisheries are being overfished.

Although other factors, such as ocean pollution, reef damage, and wetland destruction, contribute to fish stock depletion, overharvesting is the principle cause. With improved technology, such as radar, spotter planes, and bigger nets and lines, fishers are able to catch more fish at a lower cost. Trawling nets large enough to swallow 12 jumbo jets in a single gulp, long-lines stretching for 75 miles with thousands of hooks, and huge drift-nets are some of the modern tools that contribute to overharvesting. But despite the enhanced fish-catching capability, the principle cause lies elsewhere. The lack of fish ownership is what causes overfishing. Virtually no incentive to conserve is evident since any fish saved will simply get caught and sold by someone else.

Fishers are supplying what consumers are demanding. When a single bluefin tuna can sell for $80,000 or more, is it any wonder that fishers are fishing this species to extinction? Because fishing capability has improved, fish populations are overharvested, and catches, as well as profits, decline. With increasing world demand for fish and no fish-protected property rights, there simply are not enough fish in the sea any longer.

Another reason that resources might be misused is because private returns from an investment may be less than the social return. For instance, an owner of a wetland may choose to fill in the wetland in order to build houses that can be sold for a profit (private return). On the other hand, wetlands purify water, mitigate flooding, and provide valuable habitat (social returns). Although the benefits to society may be greater if the wetland is preserved, the private owner may not be able to charge those who benefit from the wetland to cover his or her costs in preserving it; consequently, the private owner makes the decision to fill it in. This is the problem of the public good discussed earlier.

Solving the Problem of Resource Misuse

Unspoiled scenery, biodiversity, or unique ecosystems such as barrier islands often suffer from pollution and overdevelopment. Historically, we have relied on the government to take over control and protect our valuable resources. The federal government began preserving wild areas in 1872 when it established Yellowstone National Park.[4] Federal laws also protect endangered species (animal and plant life) by limiting what private citizens can do with their property.

However, governmental regulation of common pool resources has not always led to cries of "bravo" and "encore." The sounds more often sound like "hiss" and "boo." A case in point is the halibut fishery off the coast of Alaska. The government regulated the overfished resource by restricting the *time period* that halibut could be caught. The government shortened a season that had previously run four months, to just a few days, thinking that a shorter fishing season would lead to fewer fish caught. However, the new rules caused the existing stock to be fished more intensively, resulting in too much effort and cost, just as economic theory (and common sense) would predict. Too many boats crowded the area, and boats scurried about to catch as much as possible in the limited time. The frenzied harvest resulted in not only higher netting costs for the fishers who needed bigger boats and more equipment, but also higher processing costs because large processing and storage capacity was required. Because the halibut was frozen, the quality was also diminished, resulting in tasteless patties rather than fresh fish.[5] The results didn't make anyone happy. A recent license and compensation scheme has led to some improvement in the halibut fishery. Similar misfortunes abound with government regulation of other fisheries.

In recent years we have come to realize that there are other ways, often more efficient and productive, of protecting resources. One option is for the government to increase fishing costs, which will lead to fewer fish caught. For example, in Maryland's portion of the Chesapeake Bay, fishers cannot dredge for oysters with motorized power. This is a form of regulated inefficiency, which decreases catches but creates higher costs than necessary for society.

A better alternative would be a policy that limits the number of fish caught and actually lowers the cost. An Individual Transferable Quota (ITQ) system that gives a fisher the right to catch a portion of the total allowable catch does just that. Say we wish to harvest one million tons of salmon each year while maintaining the total stock of fish at current levels. If there were 1,000 salmon fishers, each fisher could be given a permit to catch 1,000 tons of fish annually. The fish population would be protected for future generations, and fishers could use any means they chose in catching their permit quota. Such a policy controls access, and because the permit is transferable, that is, can be sold, high-cost fishers exit the market by selling their quotas to lower-cost fishers. In 1986, New Zealand started the first ITQ program, and other nations, including the United States, Canada, Iceland, the Netherlands, and Australia, have followed suit. A well-defined property rights system encourages owners to protect common property resources.

Privatization has worked very well with some species of fish and shellfish. Aquaculture, or fish farming, protects many fish that previously were subject to overuse. Farm-raised salmon account for about half (in 1996) of the world's salmon sales, which is an increase from 7% a decade ago.[6] Most catfish sold in restaurants and fish markets are raised in private ponds. Clearly, some fish and animals are easier than others to own and protect.

Earlier, we discussed how for centuries Swiss farmers have shared a pastureland without overusing it because access to the resource was controlled. Other examples of resources that are owned in common yet not ruined because of agreed-upon constraints include lobster fisheries in Maine, the Nijukiine Forest in Kenya, and coral reefs in the Philippines where each family is given property rights to a portion of the reef.

Private groups, like the Nature Conservancy, are part of a market solution to the problems of resource misuse. The Nature Conservancy, which protects biodiversity by buying sensitive ecosystems, controls 10 million acres in the United States and 1 million acres in Latin America and the Caribbean. Additionally, the Conservancy has established a number of conservation programs in Pacific Island nations and Indonesia. Other environmental groups, such as the Palmetto Conservation Foundation, buy wilderness in open markets and set it aside for posterity, thereby bidding the resource away from other potential uses such as for housing or pulpwood.

Markets encourage natural resource conservation in other ways. Developers recognize the profitability of housing developments where trees are protected, green space is preserved, population density is reduced, and wildlife is protected. Developers spend a lot of money to preserve natural amenities because buyers value environmental amenities.

In 1991, an investment group bought and began developing Dewees Island, just north of Charleston, South Carolina, with the intent of selling residential lots but at the same time providing certain environmental amenities. The natural environment of Dewees Island is being preserved by draconian restrictions endorsed by none other than the property owners themselves. Automobiles are not allowed on the island; no concrete or asphalt can be used on roads or walkways; only plants and trees native to the island can be used for landscaping; and only organic pesticides or herbicides are tolerated. Yet, buyers pay higher prices than normal for the property, reflecting the value that the buyers place on environmental goods. Here we have a good example of a private, for-profit group that protects environmental goods. Buyers clearly value the natural environment over some modern conveniences.[7]

Dewees is not an isolated case. Other South Carolina barrier islands have their own environmental plans. Kiawah, Seabrook, Daufuskie, and Debordieu are privately developed islands that sell buyers on environmental protection well in excess of any state or federal laws. On all of these islands, and many others in other states, the cost of land and building construction is elevated because of the requirements to protect trees, vegetation, sand dunes, and wildlife.

Private markets are also actively supporting the protection of wildlife, wetland, and wilderness in other ways. Many private landowners have come to realize that it is profitable to abandon the growing of regular crops, trees for lumber and pulp, and cattle, and provide recreational experiences for a fee. Hunters are willing to pay a fee for access to these lands. Hikers and campers are willing to pay for a wilderness experience. Fishermen are willing to pay to wet a hook in a private lake or river.

The desire to preserve natural environments and wilderness areas increases as natural areas become scarcer. As John Krutilla said, wild places are "irreplaceable assets of appreciating value with passage of time."[8] Because we value wild places, we want to expend resources to protect these areas. Beautiful, natural environments attract people and businesses, oftentimes creating greater value for society than if wilderness areas were used for lumber, roadways, and housing.

While market prices do a good job of mitigating resource scarcity, they don't necessarily do a good job of mitigating damage to the environment from the extraction, processing, and use of natural resources. In cases where mining and other resource industries scar the land and leave behind toxic waste, or resource use creates environmental pollution, we must consider methods to control the problem. Mining activities scar the land and pollute land and water with acid runoff. Processing ore has created large dead zones in places like Ducktown, Tennessee, and Sudbury, Ontario. And when we use resources like fossil fuels we create air pollution. We discuss these issues further in upcoming chapters.

Summary

Dramatic predictions of impending resource depletion and doom make good headlines, but they are invariably incorrect and distract us from constructive policymaking to deal with the resource problems that are real. Generally, natural resources are overused and misused in those situations where property rights are not well-defined and protected, and markets are not allowed to work. If allowed to operate properly, markets can be effective at preserving and protecting resources for future generations. And with appropriate understanding and government action, markets can be made to work even better.

Some previous skeptics now agree that markets often do a good job of reducing concerns of resource loss. Paul Ehrlich states that, "for many nonrenewable resources, the main problem in the next few decades will be not their exhaustion . . ." Also, Ehrlich admits that he "may have undervalued the amount of technological innovation and substitution that can be called forth in the short term by prices driven by scarcity."[9] Others agree, including the Club of Rome, which admitted, "it is highly improbable that physical limits to man's limits will ever be reached" recognize the ability of humans to adjust.[10] The lesson is clear: We should continue to study, evaluate, and promote market-oriented solutions to natural resource protection.

If we pulled a Rip van Winkle and fell asleep today, and woke up one hundred years from now, what resources would be missing? We might prognosticate that if markets were allowed to continue to operate, we could find pools of oil, veins of coal, and forests of trees still available. However, we won't see many species of plants and animals that we currently enjoy, unless we change our current actions. We discuss biodiversity loss and offer some possible solutions in chapter 6.

Chapter 6

‿‿

Where Be the Dragons?:
Biodiversity Loss

Nature makes nothing in vain.

—Aristotle

Although *Jurassic Park* was a blockbuster movie, the premise that we can bring back an extinct species is not reality. Once we lose a species we can't bring it back. Extinction is irreversible. And we've been losing a lot lately. Natural extinctions have always occurred as species failed to adapt to changing conditions, but at a slower rate than is the current situation. Today, human actions cause most extinctions. Estimates of the current rate of species extinction are difficult to calculate, but biologists say that species are vanishing at a rate of 100 to 1000 times faster than before humans existed.[1]

Much of the biodiversity we lose is still a mystery to us. As E. O. Wilson puts it, we live on an unexplored planet. We know of perhaps only 10% of existing species on earth and continually discover new species and new uses of species. Furthermore, we know very little about many of the species we have identified. Until a few years ago, the Pacific yew tree was considered a nuisance to be burned when old growth forests were harvested. A chemical from the yew tree is now used to shrink tumors. Scientists are just beginning to study many ocean species.

The Value of Biodiversity

Biodiversity, which is the variety of ecosystems, plants, animals, and microorganisms, is valuable for ethical, ecological, aesthetic, spiritual, and commercial reasons. Some make the argument that each species has an inherent right to exist, regardless of its usefulness to humans. Ecologically, genetic variability among individuals, within a species, and among the number of species is valuable because it creates balance and stability in an ecosystem.

The economic value of biodiversity includes use and nonuse value. We harvest many natural resources such as fish, game, and lumber. Various species provide agricultural, industrial, and pharmaceutical products. Twenty-five percent of new medicines originate in a tropical rain forest, and we continually find new products in the wild. Many staple crops, such as the potato, have been given genetic characteristics that make them resistant to cold, disease, and drought, by finding and researching various species of wild potatoes in remote areas of the Andes mountains. St. Johns Wort, a popular herb substitute, and Prosac come from a common weed that covered vast areas of California and Washington.

Ecotourism is growing rapidly in many nations and generates an estimated $30 billion a year. Tourists are increasingly visiting ecosystems that provide wildlife viewing. Ecotourism captures some of the willingness to pay for preserving wildlife.

Other benefits from protecting habitat include nonmarket benefits such as carbon sequestration from forests, and water purification and flood mitigation from wetlands. Also, we discussed in chapter 4 nonuse benefits such as existence, option, and bequest value. Although these values are difficult to measure, they should be included if we are to make wise policy choices.

Why We Destroy Biodiveristy

Several factors contribute to the loss of biodiversity. Although overharvesting and competition from nonnative species is the cause of some species extinction, habitat conversion is the principle cause of biodiversity loss. Many species range over a limited habitat range, and when that habitat is destroyed the species disappears. Loss of tropical forest, where 50% to 90% of the earth's terrestrial species live, is especially costly. In recent decades the rate of tropical deforestation has accelerated. Each year tropical forests the size of the state of Florida are destroyed. To understand the reasons for the current rapid rate of extinction, we must explain why we destroy habitat.

Activities such as farming, mining, forestry, grazing, water impoundment, and urbanization destroy habitat. When we undertake such activities, we often don't take into account the full cost of the actions. Because biodiversity and the benefits provided by biodiversity, such as water purification, are public goods, the market will not provide the incentive to preserve the desirable amount. If the owner is not paid for the benefits of a wetland (for example, water purification and flood mitigation) but is paid to fill the wetland to build houses, we should not be surprised that the owner paves over the wetland. Although the social benefits from protection may be greater than the private benefits from conversion, because the full benefit of the wetland cannot be appropriated by the owner, the wetland may be destroyed. And who will pay a nation to protect a rain forest for the carbon sequestration benefits?

Governments often subsidize habitat conversion, sometimes because of government development priorities, but more often because of political lobbying by special interest groups such as farmers and loggers. A major cause of deforestation is conversion to alternative uses, especially agriculture. In recent years the rate of slash-and-burn agriculture has been increasing due to population migration to forested areas, short-term oriented policies, and poorly defined property rights.

Biodiversity often is not protected because of a lack of property rights. Open-access harvesting of common pool resources, such as elephants, rhinoceri, and leopards leads to their extinction. The introduction of a nonnative species into a system where they are not native can also cause the extinction of a species. British colonists introduced the Nile perch into Lake Victoria in East Africa in order to improve fishing. Within 20 years the predator fish eliminated nearly half of the 400 native fish species. The accidental introduction of rats and snakes caused the extinction of many island bird populations in New Zealand.

Some habitat is destroyed as a side effect of human activity. Runoff from urbanization and farming destroys aquatic habitat, and boater recreational use, such as scuba diving and fishing, may destroy coral reef. No one person factors in the cost imposed on others of spilled gasoline, pesticides used in the garden, or a boat anchor that breaks off a piece of coral.

The Endangered Species Act

In the United States, the Endangered Species Act (ESA), an ambitious and controversial piece of legislation, is primary legislation designed to protect important species and habitat. The original ESA of 1969 authorized the Secretary of the Interior to purchase land for species protection and preservation. The ESA, passed by Congress in 1973, protects habitat and also contains a provision for listing species as "threatened" or "endangered."

The ESA is a command-and-control approach that limits what property owners can do with their land. Under the present set of federal laws it is a crime to harm endangered species, which often precludes the property owner from using his or her land in the most profitable way. Harm includes significant habitat modification and degradation in a manner that injures or kills a listed species. If an endangered specie is found, the property owner is required to protect the endangered specie at the owner's expense, even if it means a complete loss of property value. Consequently, most property owners don't survey their land for endangered species. Being realistic about it, it is better not to know if an endangered species is on your property. If an endangered species is discovered, a sudden disappearance would be in the property owner's personal interest. Consider the case of the Delhi Sands fly.

Mark Twain said "Nothing was made in vain, but the fly comes near it." Maybe so, but we find the Delhi Sands fly on the Endangered Species list. The Delhi Sands fly, which is about an inch long and is spotted with dabs of orange and brown, lives for about a week. In 1993 plans to build a hospital, 300 jobs for the project, and hopes to attract business and government into a depressed area near Los Angeles were held up because of the Delhi Sands Fly. A coalition of property rights activists, developers, and farmers are presently challenging the ESA with a lawsuit. Defenders of the fly contend that the fly is "part of a healthy ecosystem, and when species start dying, it's a clear sign that something's wrong."[2]

Unfortunately, for these reasons, the ESA has protected habitat ineffectively, especially on privately-owned property. Of the 711 species listed since 1973, less than 10% are improving, 20% are stable, almost 40% are declining, and the status of about 30% is uncertain.[3] Years ago Aldo Leopold recognized that "Conservation will ultimately boil down to rewarding the private landowner who conserves the public interest."[4] Because most endangered species habitat is on private land, cooperation from property owners is imperative for protection of biodiversity. In South Carolina, for example, 90% of the state's land is privately owned.

The ESA sometimes has the unintended result of punishing good land stewardship. Landowners who provide good habitat can have their land literally "taken" away by the government. Consequently, a landowner may preemptively, and legally, destroy habitat if no endangered species currently occupies the property. The well-documented case of Ben Cone in North Carolina illustrates the effects of the disincentives created by the ESA. Cone had managed his 7,200 acres of forest in the North Carolina Sandhills region for quail hunting, which also provided ideal habitat for red-cockaded woodpeckers, an endangered species. The owner was faced with the complete loss of the value of his timber because the government, in the interest of protecting the birds, would not allow the owner to cut his timber. "I cannot afford to let those woodpeckers take over the rest of the property. I'm going to start massive clearcutting," said Ben Cone, the owner of the property. Although Cone would have preferred to maintain the open habitat forest, he dramatically increased his old growth pine harvesting to avoid potential RCW habitation and subsequent ESA limitations.[5]

The framers of the U.S. Constitution recognized the importance of private property when they put in the "takings clause" in the 5th amendment. Based on the "takings clause," if a branch of government appropriates a private person's land for public use, the owner must be compensated for the market value of the property. If local government takes a person's property for a sewer line, for instance, the owner is paid. Historically, the U.S. Supreme Court only recognized a 100% taking. A partial taking could occur and government may not be obligated to compensate the owner.

Often value is taken even if land is not physically taken. This occurs, for example, when the government does not allow a property owner to log the land because an endangered species is found. A "regulatory takings" occurs when the title to the land is not taken away, but its use is taken. If the primary use is for the land's timber and cutting trees is denied, the property owner has lost most of the value of the property, and it should surprise no one if the owner does everything in his or her power to avoid the loss, even eliminating endangered species.

With the 1992 decision of the U.S. Supreme Court in the Lucas case, we may be on the verge of a radical change. Lucas in 1986 bought two lots in Wild Dunes on the Isle of Palms near Charleston, South Carolina. As a builder and developer, his intention at the time was to build houses on the lots for sale. At the time he purchased the lots for slightly less than $1 million, his intended use was perfectly legal. However, the state of South Carolina changed its building set-back requirements in 1988. As it turned out, most of Lucas' lots were seaward of the new set-back lines, making his land virtually worthless. Lucas sued the state, where he prevailed in the circuit court, but was overturned by the South Carolina Supreme Court. Lucas appealed to the U.S. Supreme Court where he got a favorable ruling. The state compensated Lucas.[6] This case and other court decisions have encouraged property owners in their attempts to get compensated for partial takings. If government is required to compensate property owners in other circumstances when regulation causes property loss, this may limit environmental regulation, including endangered species protection.

In light of takings challenges and poor results of the ESA, some changes are being introduced so that the property owner is not the sole bearer of the cost of an action that benefits all citizens. Some state laws now require compensation for land owners for partial takings. Also, policymakers are seeking compromise with landowners. Recently the government created the "safe harbor" project to encourage property owners to protect the red cockaded woodpecker (RCW). The RCW inhabits mature pine forests of the southern coastal plain from southern Virginia south to Florida and west to Texas. Despite protection as an endangered species since 1970, the RCW has continued to decline throughout its range, especially on private land, where much of the its habitat is located. Of the estimated one million groups that existed in the mid-1800s, perhaps 5,000 groups remain. The loss, degradation, and fragmentation of habitat is the primary cause of RCW decline.

In order to encourage private landowners' cooperation, ecologists and economists with the Environmental Defense Fund, together with Fish and Wildlife Service personnel, developed the RCW Safe Harbor Program (SHP). In return for agreements by private landowners to create, restore, or enhance habitat for endangered species, the government will not place future restrictions on what they may do with their land if additional RCWs are attracted to the area. Individuals can also opt out of the agreement. Basically, the landowner is no longer penalized for doing a good deed. Also, the SHP requires the landowner to actively manage habitat that is necessary for the survival of the RCW, unlike the ESA which only obligates landowners to avoid a "take."

As of November 2000, 47 landowners have enrolled 142,764 acres of habitat and 190 woodpecker groups in the SHP. The properties are in 12 South Carolina counties located in the state's coastal plain. Almost one-half of the state's RCWs are currently protected under the SHP. Pending the expected approval of two new enrollees, almost 100% of RCWs on private land will be included in the program. Participants include large industrial landowners, small private landowners, and public landowners. SHP enrollees use the land for quail plantations, forestry operations, golf courses, and residential use. Although three years is too brief a period to evaluate a policy that relates to extinction, the SHP offers considerable promise as a program that encourages private landowners to practice habitat conservation. A program such as the SHP is necessary for species such as RCWs that require habitat enhancement for recovery.[6]

Researchers are considering species as parts of ecosystems rather than independent entities. There may also be economies of scale to this type of approach. Current (1998) bills in the House and Senate contain elements of a multi-species approach.[7]

Other Policies to Protect Biodiversity

When people convert tropical forests and other habitat for expected economic benefit, they weigh personal gain against personal cost, not taking into account cost imposed on others. To preserve biodiversity, we must implement policies that force individuals to factor in the costs imposed on others, penalize activities that destroy species and habitat, and reward those who protect biodiversity.

Some species are valuable as pharmaceuticals, such as those found in rain forests. If a country and its citizens could share in the profits made from such uses, they would have more of an incentive to protect the rain forest. For example, the Costa Rican government allows the Instituto Nacional de Biodiversidad to contract with pharmaceutical companies to prospect and develop genetic resources for a fee. The first agreement was with Merck, the world's largest pharmaceutical company, for $1 million over two years.[8] Incentive systems such as these should be expanded.

The Guyanan government is attempting another trial program.[9] The Guyanan government is currently protecting a large preserve of virgin forest that protects valuable ecosystems and many endangered species. Because Guyana is a poor country, with 80% of the population below the poverty level, protecting the preserve is an expensive proposition. Allowing timber companies to cut the trees would create many well-paying jobs. For long-term forest protection it is clear that income-generating alternatives must be created. The government hopes that funds from international groups, ecotourism, and sustainable harvesting of some plants will provide enough revenue to justify the trial program. Other proposed revenue programs include fish farming and selling pharmaceutical companies the rights to plants that may produce new drugs. If a recent study that suggests that the value of biodiversity prospecting may not generate enough economic value for long-term protection is correct, other approaches will also be necessary.[10]

Issuing carbon credits to help limit global warming could provide the incentive to protect large tracts of tropical forest. Because trees absorb carbon, nations may pay nations that preserve large tracts of forest. We will return to the idea of carbon sinks when we discuss global warming in chapter 8.

Debt-for-nature swaps can also be useful policy. Under this program, a conservation agency buys up some of a developing nation's international debt. The conservation agency then forgives the debt in return for a promise that a conservation area such as a national park will be protected. Debt-for-nature swaps have been transacted in Bolivia, the Philippines, Zambia, among other places.

Better-defined property rights could help control open-access harvesting. An innovative experiment with elephant property rights offers some encouraging results. Elephant herds have declined because of illegal hunting to obtain ivory. Tribes also kill elephants because they damage crops and property and occasionally kill people. In some African countries the government gives villages' property rights to the elephants. Since villagers receive benefits from the herd in the form of payments from tourists viewing the elephants and limited harvesting of ivory, villagers work to protect the elephants from poachers. If the elephants are hunted to extinction, villagers lose long-term benefits. The government also compensates villagers for any damage done to crops by elephants. Elephant herds are increasing in countries that provide some community ownership such as Zimbabwe, Botswana, Namibia, and South Africa, while herds are decreasing in Kenya, a country without private incentives.

The 1975 Convention on International Trade In Endangered Species (CITES) is an important international treaty with the goal of halting the trade of endangered species. However, if the species is common property, more hunting, not less, will likely result. Because the trade is illegal, the price for the species increases, and poachers increase their activities because of the increased profits.

Other incentive programs encourage species protection in the United States. Since 1987, The Defenders of Wildlife have been paying ranchers for the costs (dead sheep and cows) caused by wolves. Sometimes species are protected because of market demand. Hunters pay farmers to reserve their land for hunting. The Delta Waterfowl Foundation pays farmers to protect waterfowl nesting habitat. While some animals are hunted and killed, great pains and costs are incurred to preserve the animals for future use. Food and habitat are maintained, and in the process other wildlife are protected as well. In other cases property owners protect wildlife and habitat for aesthetic reasons.

Private organizations such as the Nature Conservancy buy threatened ecosystems. The organization uses private and corporate donations to buy ecologically important areas threatened by development. Since 1951 the Nature Conservancy bought over 11,000 square miles in the United States and 31,000 square miles of wildlife habitat outside of the United States.

Other financial incentives for landowners fall into a broad range, including estate tax reforms, tax relief for easements or donations, bounties for attracting rare species, and outright compensation. Some states provide financial incentives to landowners. Policymakers in Florida are implementing a resource conservation agreement that provides compensation (e.g., Federal tax incentives) to landowners in exchange for an agreement to maintain and manage natural habitats and/or agricultural lands for the Florida panther (FL-panther.com). South Carolina passed an Endangered Species Incentive Act in 1999, which offers financial incentives to property owners who protect endangered species habitat. The Act provides up to $5 million of income tax credits for each South Carolina taxpayer who incurs costs for "habitat management or construction and maintenance" for threatened or endangered species.

Mitigation banking, another recent program, allows landowners to earn credits that can be sold to others who need to mitigate for adverse impacts to the species. The U.S. Fish and Wildlife Service (FWS) supervises a mitigation credit market for some species, including the RCW. After the FWS completes a survey to determine the baseline number of RCW, nonbaseline RCW groups may be sold as mitigation credits to landowners who wish to destroy RCW habitat. Mitigation sites must have sufficient continuous pine habitat to support at least ten RCW groups and have approved habitat management plans including regular prescribed burning and cavity management. The landowner "selling" the credit accepts the responsibility of protecting the additional nonbaseline RCW.[11]

And a final, and familiar policy to improve biodiversity protection—STOP GOVERNMENT SUBSIDIES for activities that destroy habitat. For example, below-cost timber sales, agricultural subsidies, flood insurance, and depletion allowances for mining all encourage activities that contribute to habitat and species loss. O'toole estimates that more than half of all extinctions in the United States are tied to government-subsidized activities.[12]

Summary

On occasion, private property owners sometimes contribute to habitat preservation, sometimes knowingly and sometimes unintentionally. In South Carolina, a longleaf pine-wiregrass habitat area that included a gopher tortoise colony was discovered on private property. Due to development, agriculture, and highway construction, a gopher tortoise colony is a rare find these days. Why was this particular habitat protected? Several generations of bootleggers actively kept all trespassers off to protect their investment in moonshine. Inadvertently they protected a valuable resource for society.[13] Recently, the South Carolina Heritage Trust Program has acquired the land and will protect this valuable habitat.

One long-term remedy may well lie in further education of the world in the benefits of biodiversity. Greater appreciation for the value of biodiversity will create more incentive to protect it. Biodiversity provides much value for humankind, and understanding the economic value of conservation and the economic factors that cause biodiversity loss will help to acquire international support for protecting biodiversity. Society will preserve species and resources as long as society values such things and is willing to pay the price of preservation. Market approaches such as sustainable harvesting can encourage human actions that preserve biodiversity.

Catastrophic events, such as volcanic eruptions or asteroids crashing into the earth can create an abrupt rise in extinction rates. Five mass extinctions have occurred over the past 500 million years, each event wiping out perhaps three-fourths of all species at that time. For the first time a species, *Homo Sapiens*, is responsible for large-scale extinctions. When environmental conditions change, a species either adapts or becomes extinct. *Homo Sapiens*, a resourceful and adaptable species, has thrived. Our resourcefulness will be put to the test if we are to preserve species endangered by human actions.

Chapter 7

〜〜

I Get Along without You Very Well: Solving Pollution Problems

As important as technology, politics, law, and ethics are to the pollution question, all such approaches are bound to have disappointing results, for they ignore the primary fact that pollution is primarily an economic problem, which must be understood in economic terms.

—Larry E. Ruff

Today everybody is downwind or downstream from somebody else.

—William Ruckelshaus

In the sci-fi movie *Blade Runner*, in 2019 Los Angeles is a dismal place: the sun never shines; rain falls continually; and the polluted air makes you cough. Sounds like Pittsburgh in the summer of 1969, when steel mills were spewing pollution and people were driving with car headlights burning in the middle of the day to see through the thick smog. Pittsburgh is much improved today and is now often rated as one of the most "livable" cities in the country. Given our current environmental problems, can we hope to avoid a *Blade Runner* world and enjoy a renaissance like Pittsburgh?

It's a physical law that energy and matter cannot be destroyed; production just rearranges it. When we use natural and human resources to produce the goods we desire, we create wastes that often damage the environment. When businesses and consumers shift some of the cost of production onto nonconsenting third parties, we suffer what is called a negative externality leading to a serious underestimate of the real cost of production.

Early environmental laws, such as the 1970 Clean Air Act, set air quality standards so high that in theory, at least, *no one anywhere* in the United States would suffer ill effects from air pollution. And cost didn't matter. Similarly, the 1972 Clean Water Act was designed to eliminate *all* discharge into navigable waters by 1985. Over time, we have come to realize that these weren't realistic goals.

In this chapter we deal with the question as to what is an acceptable level of pollution. In other words, how much pollution should we control? We also explore alternative environmental policies in search of the ones that best help us reach our goals.

How Much Pollution is OK?

Chemical acronyms such as PCBs, CFCs, and DDT are commonplace. Modern society has created an alphabet soup of toxic chemicals that we dump into our air, water, and soil. According to the American Chemical Society, 15,000,000 chemical substances are registered and in use in America. We also create innumerable tons of biodegradable waste that can be less damaging but harmful to the environment nonetheless. As Barry Commoner says, "No action is without its side effects."

Part of the pollution problem is technological, in that we just don't have the technological capability of producing goods and services pollution-free. Another part of the problem stems from the fact that unrestricted market systems encourage the production and consumption of too many goods and consequently too much pollution. Although market prices generally accurately reflect production costs, some costs, especially environmental costs, aren't taken into account by producers and consumers. As a consequence, their actions often lead to excessive environmental damage.

Examples of such occurrences are common, but consider a single illustration. An electric utility may choose to dump sulfur dioxide into the atmosphere because controlling the gas would cost money and raise the price of electricity. Yet, society suffers the cost in the form of increased levels of acid rain, which endangers human health and damages lakes, streams, vegetation, and wildlife. The low price encourages consumers to use more electricity than they would at higher prices, and even more polluted air is the result. The producers and consumers of the product bear too little of the cost of dumping waste into the air and water, and society bears too much of the cost. And, when something comes "free of charge" to a user, like clean air and water, it is likely to be used to excess. From an efficiency and equity point of view, the cost of pollution control should fall on producers and consumers of the products involved, irrespective of the pollution control policy adopted.

Pollution occurs when we produce too much waste, noise, congestion, or other things that negatively affect human well-being. The negative effects to human well-being include illnesses such as cancer, allergies, infertility, birth defects, heart disease, and less egregious things such as obnoxious odors, unsightly views, and loss of wildlife, plants, trees, water, and air quality.

Plenty of blame for environmental damage is out there for everyone. Since businesses are trying to maximize profits, they naturally try to avoid costs whenever possible. Firms must pay workers, raw material costs, and utility bills if they want to remain in business. On the other hand, firms sometimes are able to shift some costs, such as production waste, to others. The result is polluted air, land, and water. Even though firms are often vilified for such actions, the practice continues. Of course, consumers provide much of the incentive for disposing of wastes in this manner because they prefer paying low prices for products they desire. An environmentally conscious (and high cost) producer would lose business to a less environmentally conscious (low cost) producer, unless consumers willingly pay a higher price for a "green" product.

Numerous consumer activities directly and indirectly damage the environment. Such activities include driving vehicles with internal combustion engines, buying clothing made of synthetic fibers, installing and maintaining pretty green lawns that require chemical herbicides and insecticides, and hundreds of thousands of other activities that pollute the air, land, and water.

The government also contributes to environmental damage with many of their own activities, such as operating military aircraft that spew millions of tons of carbon into the atmosphere and disposing of spent uranium that threatens us all. Sadly, some environmental pollution is actually encouraged by government policy. For example, the government subsidizes, through insurance and disaster benefits, activities such as coastal development that damage the marshes, beaches, tidal creeks, and lagoons. Although it is not the intent of the government to damage the environment, it is the effect of the policy nonetheless.

Indeed, it's clear who is to blame for environmental degradation. In the immortal words of Pogo, "We have met the enemy and he is us."

How much pollution should we allow? That is the critical question. Although pollution causes negative effects to human well-being, in a world of scarce resources our goal should not be to eliminate all of it, except perhaps for the most harmful substances. For one thing, we simply don't and never will have the technological capability of eliminating all pollution. Furthermore, the environment can assimilate some amount of biodegradable waste with very low negative effects. For example, bacteria in lakes and streams break down animal waste runoff. Unfortunately, with six billion people daily spewing tons of pollutants into the water and air, in many places we have surpassed the assimilative capacity of the environment.

Another reason to allow some pollution is that the act of reducing pollution takes resources away from other important needs. Money used to clean up or prevent pollution could instead be used to build schools or hospitals or any number of thousands of other things. Also, higher pollution standards drive up production costs, which in turn drives up prices, which in turn drives down standards of living, another unappealing outcome for many, especially for those at the lowest end of the income ladder.

Pollution control can be very expensive, and can be increasingly expensive as we clean up more pollution. When government began enforcing environmental regulation in the 1970s, the first units of pollution were controlled at a low cost. After we cleaned up the easiest pollution, the costs of cleaning up additional units became much higher. For example, it can now cost $50,000 to prevent the discharge of a single ton of volatile organic compounds in Los Angeles. In the 1970s the same ton could be prevented at a cost of 50 cents.[1] While the additional costs of pollution control increase as we control more pollution, the additional benefits diminish. If the environment is very polluted, controlling 10% of the pollution provides a lot of benefit to society. However, when pollution levels are low and the environment is able to assimilate much of the pollution, that same 10% pollution reduction provides much less benefit.

Although zero pollution is not a realistic choice, we must limit pollution amounts. In theory, the question of how much pollution is acceptable can be answered rather easily: when the benefit of additional pollution control is greater than the cost of additional pollution control, we are better off by reducing the level of pollution. Conversely, if the cost of additional pollution control is greater than the benefit received, reducing pollution would make us worse off.

What this means is that the optimum level of pollution is at the point where the additional cost of controlling another unit of pollution is just equal to the additional cost of the damage from another unit of pollution. Such an equilibrium will seldom, if ever, occur where pollution is zero. For example, if industrial plants along Lake Erie pay $1 billion to reduce their effluent levels by 10%, but we gain $5 billion of benefits for recreational users and those who use the water for drinking and other purposes, then reducing their pollution by 10% is obviously a good choice. If we continue to raise pollution standards by another 10%, 20%, and 30% and so on, the cost for each additional increment of clean water will rise. The second 10% may cost $3 billion, the third 10% $6 billion, etc. Also, as the lake gets cleaner and cleaner, the marginal benefit will decline. The second 10% may produce only $4 billion in benefits, still a good thing since the cost would be less at $3 billion; but the third 10% may benefit us by only $2 billion but at a cost of $6 billion. Clearly, a bad deal.

Using this reasoning we could even show that the level of pollution should vary among pollutants and across different regions. For example, perhaps we should allow less pollution in more populated areas because the potential damage is greater than in less populated regions. We may want to restrict jet ski activity in an area where birds are nesting or allow less beach use in areas with nesting turtles. Other factors, such as weather conditions, could also affect the levels of acceptable pollution. If a temperature inversion blankets an area, a given amount of pollution may be more damaging and consequently more pollution should be reduced.

While an acceptable level of pollution can be defined in theory, it may be extremely difficult to do in practice. Lack of accurate, unassailable data from other scientists,u= such as biologists, geologists, and pathologists, as to the actual degree of harm caused by polluted air and water makes that job difficult. Evidence of pollution damage is often not conclusive because of uncertainties about how much pollution the environment can absorb or how harmful pollutants really are. Also, many things are simply very difficult to measure quantitatively, as we saw in chapter 5. Not surprisingly, business leaders and environmentalists often disagree on the extent of damage from pollution and the cost of controlling pollutants, leaving us in a quandry as to the appropriate legislative action.

Controlling Pollution:
The Case for Market Incentives

The traditional method used by the government to deal with pollution is the "command and control" approach. Because the government uses its power of command and control to set the environmental standards that polluters must follow, this method is also known as the standards approach. For example, the Environmental Protection Agency (EPA) might require a specific type of technology such as a smokestack scrubber for a paper mill, or an emission standard in the form of a limitation on the quantity of any pollutant a specific source can emit. The government could ban an activity all together, such as not allowing the construction of a fishing pier in a marsh or the filling in of a wetland. Companies that violate standards are penalized, usually with fines.

Standards tend to be inflexible and more costly than necessary. This shortcoming is illustrated by the case of the EPA requiring oil refineries to reduce benzene. The standards required Amoco to build a $41 million enclosed canal and water treatment system to capture benzene vapors. A joint study by Amoco and the EPA (cooperation between a firm and the EPA is revolutionary in itself) found the major source of benzene emissions was not where the regulation was. In fact what they found was that 97% of the benzene standard could be met with an expenditure only 25% of what was expected by installing a fairly simple device at the refinery gas pumps.[2]

As we examine alternative approaches to pollution control, keep in mind that we want to accomplish two things. First, we want to reduce pollution to an acceptable level. And second, we want to reach that goal by using least-cost methods. Although we have relied primarily on the government's standards approach to pollution control in the 1970s and 1980s, we've begun to use other ways of controlling pollution that may actually deliver better overall results. These other ways involve the use of market incentives.

One type of market incentive is an emission tax. With the tax approach, the firm pays a fee to the government for each unit of pollution it dumps into the environment. The company has a choice: reduce the level of pollution or pay the fee. The firm's managers, concerned about profits, will choose to control a unit of pollution as long as the emission tax is greater than the control cost. The tax causes the price of the firm's product to rise, which in turn causes consumers to buy less and producers to produce less. Such actions reduce pollution levels.

Now that the firm recognizes pollution as a cost like any other production cost, the firm begins to search for ways to control pollution costs. If the company pays the fee, the government can use the tax revenues to fund environmental cleanup or to compensate victims of pollution. Emission taxes represent a type of government regulation that allows firms some flexibility and incentive to find the cheapest way to control pollution. There aren't many policies that allow us to raise revenue and create a positive incentive to reduce pollution at the same time. As an added bonus, some of the revenues raised from pollution taxes could be used to lessen other taxes, such as income taxes on workers and firms.

The emission tax idea is not new. In 1920, the British economist, A. C. Pigou proposed taxing pollution as a way of internalizing pollution cost. Even before Pigou, others understood this principle and how it could be used to effectively manipulate behavior. For example, Czar Peter of Russia taxed anyone with a beard because he thought beards were uncultured and unnecessary. On the other hand Czar Peter could have used the standards approach and ordered that any bearded individual would have the beard removed along with his head. Of course, most may find the costs of execution are greater than the benefits. Perhaps the Czar recognized a low-cost solution when he saw one.

The government may have a problem determining the appropriate tax amount that would bring pollution down to the desirable level. "Is $100 per ton enough? Is $200 too much?" A trial-and-error approach may be necessary before the EPA arrives at the correct fee. But wait, we have another market incentive approach that eliminates this conundrum—the tradable permit.

Start with a government-determined acceptable level of a particular pollutant, say a million tons of sulfur dioxide per year. The government issues individual tradable permits that add up to the 1 million tons. If a firm has a permit, it is allowed to pollute up to the amount of the permit. If the firm doesn't have a permit, it can't pollute unless it buys a permit from a firm that has one for sale. The government doesn't have to set the price of the permit—the market does that through demand and supply action. The price of the permit is determined by how badly the firms want the permit (demand) and how many are available (supply). The permit can be bought and sold the same way other things are, thus insuring that the permits go to the firms with the highest needs. Even better, the firms benefit if they clean up *more* than required by the government. Firms will invest in pollution-reducing technology, thereby generating profit from the sale of unneeded permits.

A further advantage of the permit system is that it provides for a reduction in pollution levels at a lower cost than the standards approach. To illustrate, suppose there are two firms producing a total of 20 tons of sulfur dioxide (each producing 10 tons), and the government decides that we need to reduce sulfur dioxide emissions from 20 to 10 tons. The government issues two permits, each for 5 tons of sulfur dioxide and gives each firm one permit. The total pollution level will be reduced from 20 to 10 tons. The only question is: How do the firms share in the reduction? Assume that Firm A can reduce sulfur dioxide emissions by 5 tons at a cost of $5,000, while Firm B can reduce the same amount at a cost of $10,000. With a marketable permit system, Firm A could reduce its pollution by 10 tons at a total cost of $10,000 and sell its permit to Firm B for say $7,500, since it no longer needs to pollute. Firm B doesn't cut its pollution, but pays $7,500 for the additional permit it needs.

Pollution declines to the acceptable level of 10 tons as set by the government, and pollution reduction was accomplished at a total cost of $10,000 rather than $15,000. Firm A ends up with a net cost of $2,500 ($10,000 for reducing emissions by 10 tons minus $7,500 it got from Firm B when it sold its permit), which is a savings of $2,500. Firm B also saves $2,500 since it paid only $7,500 for the additional permit it bought from Firm A. To have reduced its pollution by 5 tons, the alternative to buying the permit, Firm B would have shelled out $10,000. Society gains from the permit trading since we used only $10,000 in resources to reduce the pollution by 10 tons. If the standards approach had been used, each firm would have been required to reduce sulfur dioxide emissions by 5 tons at a total cost of $15,000. Both firms and society benefit with the marketable permit system.

With marketable permits, we can set the maximum level of pollution and at the same time encourage firms to curtail their pollution by using least cost methods. Companies that can control pollution for the least cost will do so, selling their permits to those with higher control costs. If we feel that too much pollution is still being dumped, then we lower the amount of pollution even further by issuing even fewer permits. By the way, the pollution permit solution may seem familiar. In fact, this approach is the same idea as the fisheries' transferable quotas that we discussed in chapter 5.

Still Not Convinced?

Although no policy is without problems, generally market incentives offer significant benefits over the standards approach. The major problem with the standards approach is that all companies are treated the same even though pollution reduction costs are much higher for some companies than others. The market incentive approach encourages firms that can control pollution at low cost to control more pollution. Consequently, total control cost is lower. With both the emission tax and permit approach the firm determines the best method of reducing pollution, not a government agency.

The standards approach also deters innovation because it relies on penalties rather than positive incentives. If the government sets technology-based standards, companies may be aware of new and better technology that would reduce pollution even more but may "hide" it to avoid additional costs. With an incentive approach, firms are motivated to research and develop new pollution-control technology, because controlling more pollution negates the need for a permit or allows firms to escape tax liability if the tax approach is used.

Firms that can reduce pollution inexpensively will reduce even more pollution than the government requires if the proper incentives are in place. With the standards approach, the firm has no incentive to pollute less than the standard set by the government. If your company is allowed to emit 100 tons of gunk a year, why clean up any more? With a permit or tax, if the firm pollutes less, the firm buys fewer permits or pays less tax and thus saves money.

Another advantage of the permit approach is that we can be certain of the maximum amount of pollution. If 100 tons is allowable, issue 100 permits of 1 ton each. A further advantage of the permit system is that any person interested in environmental quality can buy a permit and retire it, thus reducing pollution to even lower levels than those set by the government. In fact, the National Healthy Air License Exchange (NHALE) accepts tax-deductible deductions that are used to buy and retire pollution permits.

Some complain that market incentives give firms the "license to pollute," implying that we're doing firms a favor. Senator Edward Muskie once said, "We cannot give anyone the option of polluting for a fee." He clearly implied that polluters are getting a break with this approach. But this simply is a mistaken way of viewing the problem. Even with the standards approach, firms emit pollution because everyone recognizes, including government agents, that pollution simply cannot be zero. Pollution levels would be no higher under an incentive mechanism than under a standards approach since the government can adjust tax rates and the number of permits issued in order to achieve the acceptable level of pollution. In fact, less pollution is more likely with incentives.

The acceptable level of pollution is one decision. Deciding the lowest-cost way of reaching that standard is another. Proponents of market incentives simply say, tell us how much pollution reduction society is willing to pay for, and we can offer solutions that minimize the cost that society must pay.

The EPA has implemented various incentive programs since 1975. Programs include the bubble, offset, and netting, all of which are part of the emissions trading program. However, the most important incentive system was part of the 1990 Clean Air Act (CAA). The CAA implemented tradable permits for sulfur dioxide, which is the major contributor to acid rain. Beginning in 1995, the EPA issued sulfur dioxide permits to coal-burning utilities. The amount permitted was 30% to 50% of what the companies used to pollute. By the year 2000, the total amount of sulfur dioxide emitted was 8.9 million tons per year, 10 million tons less than was emitted in 1985.[3] Originally it was expected that the permits would be traded at $500. Instead, permits are going for about $100. Such low prices indicate that firms are able to reduce sulfur dioxide at relatively low cost, thereby avoiding the necessity of buying permits. Furthermore, the permit approach encouraged firms to find the cheapest way to reduce pollution along the lines we discussed above with our examples of Firms A and B.

Analysts estimate that permit trading instituted in the 1990 Clean Air Act has lowered the annual costs of pollution reduction by $1 to $3 billion, over what it would have been with the command and control approach.[4] Because of the success of the tradable permits program, other countries such as China are beginning similar programs.

A similar permit approach has been proposed to control carbon dioxide emissions, the major contributor to global warming. In fact, the problem of global warming is a prime candidate for market incentives. (We discuss global warming in chapter 9.)

Market incentive policies can be applied to other environmental problems. Road transport is a major source of air pollution. Automobiles in the United States create about two-thirds of its carbon dioxide emissions, 90% of the carbon monoxide in urban areas and half of all atmospheric pollution. The government has issued a mandate to the State of California and 12 eastern states to encourage use of electric automobiles. By 2003, states are required to have 2–10% of all vehicles sold in the state to be electric. While this approach may lead to a reduction in air pollution, it will not be the least-cost way of doing it. Also, the costs of the mandate will be incorporated in overall car prices and effectively hidden from consumers. With an unclear connection between the benefits of cleaner air and higher auto costs, whether we get good decision making about how much pollution to eliminate is dubious indeed.

Market incentives would achieve the required air pollution reduction more efficiently through technological improvement. For example, automobile companies could be given a number of credits of allowable emissions on new automobiles. Automobile companies could then determine the least-cost way to meet the pollution reduction requirement. Automobile manufacturers may find that a cheaper way to meet the air standards is with a combination of electric vehicles, or improvements in car and engine design. Some firms may be able to reduce pollution at a lower cost and sell their unused permits, achieving the cost savings we saw in our example with Firms A and B. Incentives would also be in place to develop cleaner-burning fuels or other technology (like fuel cells) that would reduce engine emissions.

A combination of technology and market incentives would be an efficient way to control mobile-source air pollutants. Automobile drivers could be charged a fee according to how much they pollute. If a particular automobile pollutes 10% more than average, the driver might be required to pay a 10% higher tax. Such a policy would encourage automobile drivers to choose cars that produce little pollution, move closer to work and shopping, use public transportation, etc., which would decrease the amount of carbon dioxide emitted.

The Norwegian government is using a market incentive approach in the city of Trondheim to reduce congestion and urban air pollution from automobile traffic. Automobiles entering the city are charged $1.60 when drivers enter during rush hour traffic. Peak rush hour driving dropped by 10% as drivers, who now "feel the cost" of traffic externalities, consider the impact of their choice. A similar system in Singapore raises traffic tolls on days when weather conditions make pollution especially bad. To facilitate travel, the systems are fully automated. Drivers do not have to stop to pay a toll, since they are billed electronically.

In fairness, however, we should recognize that the command and control approach might be preferable in a small number of cases. If the cost of policing a permit or tax system is very high, it could be cheaper to mandate a particular pollution control technology or practice to limit pollution. In certain emergency situations, such as smog alerts in heavily polluted cities like Los Angeles, command and control may be preferable, although the Singapore road-pricing example above may be appropriate. Also, for extremely hazardous materials such as radioactive waste, for which the acceptable level is close to zero, a more direct and forceful action on the part of government may be required.

Other Solutions to Pollution Problems

Common law also provides citizens some protection from polluting firms. Lawsuits encourage economic efficiency by placing financial responsibility for environmental damage on the polluter. Consequently, firms are encouraged to practice better stewardship to avoid future legal costs. Nothing gets a business firm's attention more than having their profits and stock prices fall. Following the 1989 *Valdez* oil spill in Alaska, Exxon spent billions of dollars in cleanup costs and damage claims that otherwise could have gone to stockholders.

Ironically, the oil spill was also responsible for environmental protection. Exxon paid state and federal governments more than a billion dollars in criminal and civil damages. Some of the payments were used to purchase easements or to buy more than one-half million acres of private land, all prime habitat that might have been logged or developed otherwise. Protecting habitat may prove to be the best way to protect species.[5]

Ronald Coase, an economist and legal scholar, suggests another alternative to government regulation. According to the Coase Theorem, affected parties have an incentive to voluntarily negotiate an agreement on pollution control without government intervention if clearly defined property rights to the resource that is likely to be polluted exist. Consider the relationship between a pig farm owner and nearby neighbors. If the neighbors have the right to pollution-free streams and air, the pig farmer could not deposit waste in the air and water unless he or she paid residents for the right to pollute that air and water.

For the sake of argument, let's say the cost to the pig farmer to avoid pollution spills by building better facilities is $80,000, and the cost to the neighbors from any pig waste spills is $40,000. Under the standards approach, the EPA would simply mandate the farmer to install the facilities at a cost of $80,000 to the farmer. Yet, the result of this action is to impose a cost on society of $80,000 in the form of higher meat prices in order to save $40,000.[6] It doesn't make sense. Since the neighbors have property rights to the air and water, the two parties would negotiate a deal. The pig farmer might offer $60,000 to the neighbors if they would allow the waste to be dumped in the air and water, which means that the farmer gains $20,000 and the neighbors gain $20,000. In this case we assume no other spillover costs.

According to the Coase Theorem, if property rights are well-defined and negotiation costs are low, we may not need government intervention. If someone had secure property rights, they would have a personal, self-interest in protecting them. Clearly-defined property rights also allow better court protection via lawsuits. In practice, though, water and air are largely in the public domain. Individuals do not own water and air; consequently, no one has a personal stake in maintaining their quality. Negotiations such as those described would not be practical.

There are a number of limitations to the Coase Theorem. People may threaten to pollute just to exact a higher price or may lie about how much they are injured. If a large number of people is involved, clearly negotiations become difficult, if not impossible, to accomplish. The Coase solution is not relevant for all environmental problems, but where it is, it would be the cheapest and most equitable way of handling the problem, since it would be handled directly by the parties concerned. It is interesting to note that the permit system we discussed in this chapter is a variation of the Coase application. It is a way of privatizing air in that the permit gives the holder a property right to a particular use of the air in disposing of a pollutant. Similarly, permits to catch a certain number of pounds of fish is a way of privatizing fish.

Technology potentially offers some solutions to environmental pollution problems. Greater reliance on solar and other forms of renewable energy, such as wind and water power, would decrease carbon gases. Electric automobiles could alleviate some of the air pollution created by auto exhaust.

Sometimes Government Policy Causes Problems

How many Great Lakes are there in the United States? A good geography student would answer five— Erie, Michigan, Huron, Superior, and Ontario. Not enough according to Vermont Senator Leahy. In 1998, Senator Leahy argued that Lake Champlain, which is much smaller than the other five lakes, belongs to a different drainage system, and is in no way connected to the Great Lakes, should also be a Great lake. Why? The answer is that dubbing Lake Champlain "Great" would create benefits for Senator Leahy's constituents. And the best kind of benefits—the kind that someone else pays for. If classified as a Great Lake, Lake Champlain researchers would be eligible for $50 million annually from the federally-funded Sea Grant Program. Congress seriously considered the proposal before it was finally discarded. Although this is a minor example, there are thousands of others, all illustrating the wastefulness created by perverse incentives in the political process.

So often we enact legislation to deal with a societal problem such as an environmental one and set out with the greatest intentions only to see dismal results. In many cases the initial problem is even made worse by the new laws. The old saying that "the cure is worse than the disease" comes clearly into focus when considering such cases. A big step, often hidden, exists between the stated desired outcomes of a policy and the necessary conditions and procedures to achieve them. A cursory review of the American "war on poverty" makes our point. We have more poor today than when President Johnson started with his Great Society program and the "war on poverty" in the 1960s.

The reason the government often fails in its attempts to correct the problems so clearly identified is inherent in how democratic governments work. Voters are rationally ignorant about many things, and voters necessarily vote for candidates with a bundle of ideas. In other words, voters cannot be totally informed about all issues nor do they want to be totally informed about all issues. Second, no candidate's positions on all issues are completely compatible with a voter's views. Consequently, there is much uncertainty as to which policies will actually get legislated into law and which ones will not. And in many cases scientific evidence is pushed aside in the political battles inherent in the legislative process.

Suppose you agree with a candidate that the federal government ought to impose more control over the amount of effluent firms can release in the water and on his position on social security, but disagree with the candidate on his stand on taxes, the war on poverty, and national defense. You would no doubt have a similar experience in evaluating other candidates, some things you would agree with them on and others not. Consequently, any vote is a vote for some things you agree with and a vote for other things you don't agree with.

Complicating things even further is the fact that every person has one vote and can use that vote irrespective of the degree of benefit expected. Consider a hypothetical case. Suppose you have a community consisting of three individuals. Two of the individuals live on the left bank of the creek and the third citizen on the right bank. Say the two citizens on the left bank would gain $5,000 each if a bridge were constructed across the creek, but the right bank citizen would suffer a $20,000 loss because the bridge destroys the quiet of a wildlife preserve. The state would build the bridge using the laws of eminent domain. The two left bank residents gain $10,000 and the right bank citizen loses $20,000 for a net loss to the community of $10,000. The result is government policy that reduces human welfare and consequently is inefficient. Is there any wonder that government policy can be so uncertain, contradictory, and renders such poor results?

Democracies sometimes have trouble getting support for environmental goods because losers are seldom compensated. Majority rule means that the minority loses. Even if total benefits associated with the environmental goods exceed the costs of a majority of voters, the project will be voted down. In such cases one would expect minorities to put up a fight to protect their interests. A land use plan for Wadmalaw Island close to Charleston, South Carolina, was recently adopted by Charleston County Council. The vote was 7 to 2 to increase the number of acres per house from 5–10 acres to 7–12 acres, a move that would greatly reduce the profitability for large land owners and developers. The change in development density pleased conservationists, environmentalists, and many residents, but displeased developers and large landowners. Acrimonious discussions usually result. A compensation plan, winners paying losers, could heal many of the financial wounds associated with this plan.[7]

A further complication for democratic governments is that political candidates are deeply indebted to their financial supporters. Proponents of this or that measure are willing to invest a lot in providing the right influence to get new laws tailored and old laws changed to their liking, all at the expense of others who may be too ignorant or powerless to do anything about it. Economists and political scientists describe the special interests and legislator problem as an "Iron Triangle." The Iron Triangle is made up of politicians, government bureaucrats, and vested interest groups. Bureaucrats want to expand their budgets and influence but need the support of politicians, who in turn need the financial support of special interest groups, who in turn are clients of the government bureaucrats. Politicians use the power of government to take care of the bureaucrats and special interests, thereby ensuring their reelection, which explains the passage of legislation that a majority Americans would not support if they could vote on just that issue.

Bruce Yandle in his piece on "Bootleggers and Baptists" presents an excellent example of the political machinations that go on and why unlikely groups sometimes join together to get legislation passed. In the southern region of the United States there is a widespread government policy of preventing the sale of alcoholic beverages on Sunday. Baptists and other religious groups love it since they, on moral grounds, oppose the selling of alcohol at any time, and bootleggers also love it and "persuade politicians quietly or behind closed doors" because they have the market all to themselves on Sunday.[8] The coalition of Baptists and bootleggers makes it easy for politicians to support Sunday laws against the sale of liquor.

One environmental policy example of the bootlegger-and-Baptist theory at work was the passage of the 1977 Clean Air Act Amendments. In order to limit acid rain, the amendments required coal-fired electric-generating plants to install expensive smokestack scrubbers to remove particulate matter. Emissions could have been reduced at a much lower cost if midwestern utilities would have switched from high-sulfur coal (principally from eastern coal mines) to low-sulfur coal (principally from western coal mines). However, powerful eastern coal mine owners allied with environmentalists assured a law that required the expensive scrubbers. A victory for the bootleggers (high-sulfur coal miners) and the Baptists (environmentalists).[9]

Another disadvantage in using the government to fix things is that politicians and bureaucrats are extremely short-term oriented. They are, we suspect, short-term oriented because their constituents are short-term oriented. Most legislators have a hard time seeing beyond the next poll and the next election. Such is the nature of politics. It is true, always has been true, and always will be true. It is as natural as breathing. In any event, a short-term fixation on things provides a real disadvantage in using the government to fix long-term problems, such as environmental problems, since most are long-term by their very nature. Frank Graham notes that ". . . the initiative of government agencies in large matters of conservation is rare and generally overstated; inertia is the rule."[10]

The government may do the wrong thing, even if it knows better. The story of the snail darter and the Tellico Dam is an apt example. In 1973 the controversial Tellico Dam project in Tennessee was challenged because it was believed that damming the Tellico River would cause the extinction of the snail darter, a three-inch species of perch that subsisted on snails. Although the Endangered Species Act of 1973 ordered the protection of species regardless of costs, a provision was included in a 1978 amendment that allowed species extinction in rare circumstances if society benefited.

A special committee of government officials, the Endangered Species Committee (but better known as the God Squad) determined that the benefits of the dam were actually less than the *additional* cost of completing the project, even though the dam was already 75% completed. However, Congress appropriated funds for the project anyway and the dam was completed. Why? According to Zygmunt Platter, the environmental lawyer involved in the lawsuit, land speculators, who stood to gain a lot of money if industry moved to the area around the completed dam, influenced politicians.[11] Even when benefit-cost studies demonstrate that we are better off by protecting resources, policymakers may ignore the evidence and choose another course. The Iron Triangle strikes again.[12]

The very nature of production adversely affects the environment. For example, building a dam may uproot people and destroy flora, fauna, and habitat. Understandably, the government regulates such projects to limit the negative effects. However, some feel that in recent years regulation has become especially onerous. Along these lines, a representative from the Michigan Department of Environmental Quality recently sent a letter to a landowner threatening him with legal action because wood debris dams had been built across a stream flowing into one Spring Pond. The landowner was advised that a permit had not been acquired and that such dams caused flooding and were hazardous.

The landowner responded with the following letter:

> A couple of beavers, are in the process of constructing and maintaining two wood "debris dams" across the outlet stream of my Spring Pond. While I did not pay for, nor authorize their dam project, I think they would be highly offended that you call their skillful use of natural building materials "debris" . . . As to your dam request the beavers first must fill out a dam permit prior to the start of this type of dam activity, my first dam question to you is: are you trying to discriminate against my Spring Pond Beavers or do you require all dam beavers throughout this State to conform to said dam request? If you are not discriminating against these particular beavers, please send me completed copies of all those other applicable beaver dam permits . . . I seriously hope you are not selectively enforcing this dam policy—or once again both I and the Spring Pond Beavers will scream prejudice![13]

The State dropped the issue.

Indeed, all living things contend with scarcity and possess some ability for altering their habitat. Such is the nature of life. However, human beings have a greater capacity for altering the environment than do beavers, and the changes we make may be at a much more rapid pace than changes created by other species. On the other hand, government attempts to correct for environmental damage often leave a lot to be desired.

Summary

A common problem for modern society is that when we provide for our needs and wants, we create pollution, oftentimes with ugly consequences in human suffering. Yet, we can't have production and a level of zero pollution at the same time. Consequently, we must find an acceptable level. Our consideration of what level of pollution to allow is based on the trade-offs between benefits and costs. We rely on natural scientists to provide information on the amount of pollution and the damages that result. Through a process of weighing benefits and costs associated with any pollutant, society chooses an acceptable level.

Once an acceptable level of pollution is established, we must decide what control policy to use. A recent study concluded that although some elements of the regulatory process have worked well, overall it is often ineffective, inefficient, and excessively intrusive.[14] Historically, we have relied on a command and control approach, which basically empowers a government agency such as the EPA, to instruct business firms as to what is allowed. This approach, however, is flawed in many ways.

Policies that use market incentives, such as emission taxes and tradable permits, generally reduce pollution to acceptable levels at the least cost by allowing firms greater flexibility in employing technologies and finding alternatives. Market incentive policies such as an emission tax encourage firms to internalize the pollution costs. Internalizing the cost simply means that the firm cannot escape the tax; consequently, they cannot any longer shift the pollution cost (as measured by the tax) to third parties that are not involved with the product. The value of an incentive-based policy is that it reflects the principle that prices should include all costs. Price is a powerful force in the marketplace in that it can alter human behavior. Why not use it to help solve our pollution problems?

The United States spends a lot of money on pollution control—some $170 billion in 1997 in federal environmental regulation alone. Although we have received significant benefits from pollution control, the system can be improved. Specifically, we can get more pollution control for the dollars we are presently spending.

Market incentives are excellent policy choices for controlling pollution. They will work with any pollution control goal society sets and will provide incentives to meet that goal at the lowest cost. Some well-known environmentalists agree. Paul Ehrlich says, "Whenever possible, of course, regulation should aim to internalize externalities and minimize social costs within a market context."[15] Dave Foreman concurs: "There is little doubt about the effectiveness of environmental taxes."[16] Maybe economists and environmentalists are closer to an agreement on these important issues than some think.

We have seen significant improvements in environmental quality since the 1970s when the air pollution was thick in cities like Pittsburgh. Although the benefits of a cleaner environment may offset the unpleasant costs of regulation, we should remember that a cleaner environment comes at a cost. Higher production costs mean higher prices for consumers and goods and services available. Because the company sells less, some workers at the plant may be laid off and resource suppliers will sell less to the company. Environmental regulation was instrumental in helping Pittsburgh becoming cleaner. Of course, all of Pittsburgh's downtown steel mills closed down also. We believe that incentive-based policies will limit environmental damage to acceptable levels but at lower costs.

Chapter 8

෴

How High the Sky:
Acid Rain, Ozone Depletion,
and Global Warming

In nature there are neither rewards nor punishments—there are consequences.

—Robert G. Ingersoll

Regional or global pollutants don't recognize state or national borders. Acid rain, ozone depletion, and global warming are examples of pollutants that travel beyond local boundaries. When pollutants cross national boundaries, an already difficult problem becomes even more difficult as international agreements and cooperation become necessary. If coal-fired utilities in the American Midwest create pollutants that damage Canadian lakes and rivers, U.S. politicians may not be as diligent in finding a solution as they would be if their own constituents were being harmed.

In all three cases, solutions will require many different groups to undertake activities that are very costly. For the issues discussed in this chapter, much of the cost of inaction will be borne by future generations, while the costs of action must be paid for by the current generation. Since it is just human nature to avoid costs if possible and focus on the near term rather than the future, a further complication impedes success.

The Prehistoric Ferns Did It

"India Heat Wave Kills 2,500," "El Niños Getting Worse": Can we blame these recent (1998) events on prehistoric ferns? Maybe. We owe a lot to prehistoric plants. Fossil fuels such as oil, coal, and natural gas are the fossilized remains of prehistoric plants. We rely on fossilized plant remains to run our machinery, heat our homes, and power our vehicles. Unfortunately, as we burn fossil fuels, we release carbon dioxide (CO_2) into the atmosphere. In recent decades we've been burning more fossil fuel and consequently releasing more CO_2 into the atmosphere. And, here's the rub. Increased levels of CO_2 may contribute to global warming.

Scientists theorize that as greenhouse gases, such as carbon dioxide, methane, nitrogen oxide, and chlorofluorocarbons accumulate in the troposphere, less radiation escapes into the earth's atmosphere. There is no debate about the "greenhouse effect," which is the heat-trapping blanket over the planet that keeps the earth's temperature at a reasonable level. Without the greenhouse gases to reradiate some infrared energy back toward the earth, the oceans would be frozen solid. However, some disagreement exists among scientists as to what effect, if any, increasing levels of greenhouse gases will have on temperatures.

According to the global warming theory, the earth's surface average temperature will rise 1.5 C. to 4.5 C. by the year 2100 as a result of this increasing blanket of greenhouse gases. Human activities, especially the burning of carbon fuels such as coal, oil, natural gas, and wood, create carbon dioxide, which is the principle contributor to greenhouse gases. Scientists estimate that the concentration of carbon dioxide will double within the next 40 years. Although evidence from core drillings of the arctic ice core shows a positive correlation between carbon dioxide levels and the earth's temperature, no evidence exists to prove that one causes the other.

Although disagreement arises over how likely global warming is, the possibility that global warming may occur is a major concern and elicits considerable debate. The effects of global warming may be irreversible, and proponents of the global warming hypothesis argue that even if there's only a 50:50 chance, do we want to take a chance on ruining the planet? We will leave the debate over whether global warming will occur to the scientists. Let's assume that global warming will occur and consider the costs that would be in store for us, the costs of avoiding global warming, and what policies may help us avoid global warming. This is a job for an economist.

Global warming would create significant changes and costs for society. World-wide agricultural output would probably decline, especially in third world countries, which have fewer resources for adaptation to climate change, although some agriculture could benefit from warmer temperatures. Output in major grain belts in the United States and Europe would likely decline. Species and ecosystems would suffer, as they would not be able to adapt to the rapid change in temperature. Higher temperatures would make summers much less livable in many areas and near unbearable in congested urban areas, necessitating a greater use of air conditioning. However, some areas such as Siberia may become more livable. As the warmer temperatures cause the ice caps to melt, the sea level would rise, perhaps by some 70 centimeters. Although 70 centimeters doesn't sound like much, many island nations and many coastal areas, including productive wetlands, would be flooded. The United States would lose about 4,000 square miles of coastal land. Also, storms would likely intensify, causing greater damage to communities in proximity to the seacoast. If there are some surprises that create problems that we don't currently foresee, we could be in for even greater costs.

Although we can adapt to many of the changes resulting from global warming by migrating landward and to cooler climates, building dikes to protect shorelines, and investing in new technologies, costs would be high. Prudent people would ask: Are the likely benefits of avoiding global warming worth the costs we must incur in order to prevent it?

People from all nations dump greenhouse gases into the troposphere because it is a common pool resource. In fact, we might think of global warming as the "tragedy of the global commons." As we discussed earlier, because access to the troposphere is not controlled, users have no incentive to preserve it. Any nation that unilaterally chooses to control greenhouses gases will experience higher costs but is forced to share the benefits with others. Therefore, there is an overwhelming incentive to "ride free," that is, hope others will incur the costs while enjoying the benefits they produce. Too much pollution takes place; the commons is still spoiled, and the conscientious nation is worse off for paying to control its pollutants.

In order to reduce the likelihood of global warming, we must address two major issues: greenhouse gas reduction and rain forest protection. Although carbon gases are the major contributors to global warming, burning rain forests to clear land for agriculture also contributes significantly to global warming. Rain forests are important because trees absorb carbon dioxide; removing them leaves more carbon to be released to the troposphere. When slash-and-burn techniques cause the deforestation, we convert all the carbon stored in the tree to CO_2 immediately. Rain forests are a public good, and like all public goods, there is insufficient incentive on the part of any one person or nation to pay the price of preserving the rain forest while the rest of the world enjoys the benefits without paying a price. We may not have enough forests for carbon sequestering unless we have international cooperation, because otherwise some nations may choose to "free-ride" on other's actions.

Several factors make the global warming problem a uniquely difficult issue to resolve. Global warming would create significant costs for future generations, but the current generation must bear the cost of controlling the causes of global warming. Greenhouse gases are global pollutants, which means that their contribution to the problem is independent of their location. Toledo, Bombay, Florence—it doesn't matter where the source of the pollution is; the effects are global.

Not only is a global consensus required to control greenhouse gases, but we also must resolve the many conflicting interests of the parties involved. Policy solutions must be not only efficient (since the costs are very high) but equitable as well (each person or country should pay a "fair" share). Minimizing the cost is important, which leaves out command-and-control for reasons already discussed. If properly devised and implemented, the market incentives we discussed in chapter 7 would be the most efficient policy choice. Because greenhouse gases are global, the polluter's location does not matter; therefore, tradable permits could be an effective method to use. Countries would be allocated a certain number of permits for a given amount of pollutants that could be used or traded to other nations. This approach would be cost-effective because nations that could control gases inexpensively will do so, trading permits to nations that have a high cost of controlling greenhouse gases.

In December 1997, 5,000 delegates from 170 countries agreed to just such a policy to control greenhouse gases. The Third Conference of the Parties to the United Nations Framework Convention of Climate Change met in Kyoto, Japan, to establish international agreements to reduce greenhouse gases to deal with global warming. After intensive and lengthy negotiations, the Kyoto Protocol was adopted that would set legally binding targets on greenhouse gases.

President George W. Bush announced on March 28, 2001, that he would not send the Treaty to the Senate for ratification. The Administration's objections to Kyoto rest on the belief that the United States would face much higher energy costs and at a time when the nation already faces rising energy prices. President Bush in a letter to Senators Hagel, Helms, Craig, and Roberts, expressed his view that the Protocol was "an unfair and ineffective means of addressing global climate change concerns."[1] Apparently his view is based on the fact that Kyoto does not apply to 80% of the countries of the world, including China and India, major polluters.

However, at Kyoto Protocol meetings in July 2001 in Bonn, Germany, 178 countries (but not the United States) approved more precise rules that moved the Protocol closer to adoption. The agreement in Bonn requires the 38 industrialized countries to reduce the six greenhouse gases to 5.2% below 1990 levels for the period 2008–2012. Other important agreements were that carbon-absorbing "sinks" such as forests and farmland could be counted as reductions, and greenhouse-gas trading could be used to meet most of the reductions. The rules would go into effect when approved by legislatures of at least 55 countries, possibly by the end of 2002.

Although the Kyoto Protocol is a landmark international agreement on an extremely difficult problem, serious issues must still be resolved. William Nordhaus noted two flaws in the program negotiated in Kyoto. Only emissions from industrialized countries are limited, and tradable permits may not be a good idea because there may be great uncertainty about the price of the permits.[2]

Other problems exist. Credits to nations with carbon sinks, which refers to the uptake of gases by forest, land, and water, allow countries to actually reduce emissions by something less than the level agreed upon. This raises questions of fairness and verifiability. Also, the European Union was able to win agreement on the "bubble concept," which allows groups of countries, such as the European Union countries, to jointly meet emission standards, even though one or more members of the group is deficient. The language describing the bubble is in very general terms and allows all parties to the Kyoto agreement to engage in bubble arrangements.

Bruce Yandle suggests a coalition of Baptists (environmental groups) and bootleggers (industries and governments) are promoting the Kyoto Protocol.[3] According to Yandle, the environmental groups take the high moral ground road in pushing support for the treaty. The bootleggers are the special interest groups who stand to gain or lose personally from the Koyoto agreements. Here we find governments, industries, and firms. The developing countries expect to gain as the limits on carbon emissions apply mostly to developed countries. Coal interests lose, solar interests gain, and so on.

Some experts caution that given the uncertainties about global warming, the high cost of controlling greenhouse gases, and our ability to adapt to temperature change, we should for now impose no more than modest restrictions. Nordhaus estimates that reducing greenhouse gases by 10% would cost $2.2 billion per year, while a 30% reduction would cost $49.5 billion annually. Nordhaus and others suggest that we implement "no-regret" policies that will reduce greenhouse gases, but which will also provide benefits to society independent of global warming. For example, we could stop subsidies that contribute to inefficient deforestation, especially in South America. In the United States and other nations, depletion allowances that subsidize fossil fuel extraction could be removed. Also, a modest tax on oil could be imposed, which will improve air quality, in addition to reducing carbon gases. Polluters could be required to pay a fee for each unit of pollution emitted, thereby internalizing pollutant cost. For example, taxes on oil would increase the price of oil, decrease the amount of oil consumed, and the amount of carbon gas produced. Finally, subsidizing an urban tree-planting program would sequester carbon and improve urban air quality and aesthetics.[4] The city of Chicago is presently undertaking a program of planting trees and other plants on the roofs of all public buildings to improve air quality.

Programs to encourage the protection of major carbon sinks such as rain forests may be effective. For instance, the international community could pay Brazil to preserve areas of the Amazon rain forest. Based on the amount of damage that would be avoided by the carbon sequestering element of a forest, a 126,000 hectare forest the size of Cameroon's Korup National Park might be worth as much as $504 million.[5]

Technology, particularly photovoltaics, may mitigate carbon emissions. Although solar energy is still an expensive energy source, a recent study suggests that solar energy could be price competitive with other energy sources within 30 years. The profit motive is at work here in encouraging entrepreneurs to develop new ideas that society values.

Acid Rain, Acid Rain, Go Away

In the early 1970s dilution was the solution for some pollution problems. If a coal-burning utility was emitting more sulfur dioxide than permitted by pollution standards, a taller smokestack was the ticket. Local air pollution decreased as the pollutant was injected into the upper atmosphere where prevailing winds blew the pollutant 200 to 600 miles away. Utilities and industrial plants in midwestern states did this routinely and the pollutants—nitrogen oxides, sulfur dioxide, and chloride—combined in the atmosphere to form acid rain, which fell on northeastern states and Canada. Acid rain damages cultural resources and materials, trees and crops, aquatic life in lakes and rivers, impacts human health, and impairs visibility. Doesn't make for good neighbors, does it? Because acid rain affects more than just the vicinity of the emissions, it is known as a regional pollutant.

Acid deposition or acid rain as it is commonly known is acidic pollution falling from the sky in the form of gases, solid particles, or rain. Acid deposition delivers acids and acidifying compounds to the earth's surface, which then adversely affects ecosystems by moving through the soil, vegetation, and surface waters. Although rain is naturally slightly acidic, the rain in some eastern states can be about ten times more acidic than normal.

In 1980 the U.S. Congress funded a ten-year study, the National Acid Precipitation Assessment Program (NAPAP), to gather more information on the extent and effects of acid rain. Although the study concluded that there was insubstantial evidence that acid deposition caused the decline of trees other than red spruce trees at high-elevation, more recent evidence shows that acid deposition has contributed to the decline of red spruce trees throughout the eastern

United States and sugar maple trees in central and western Pennsylvania. Researchers are calling for an additional 40% to 80% reduction in electric utility emissions of sulfur beyond the levels set by the 1990 CAA. Also, they suggest that emission trading for nitrogen should be established.[6]

Congress passed the 1990 Clean Air Act, a major new piece of legislation to control the pollutants contributing to acid rain, as well as other pollutants. The CAA specified a 10 million ton annual reduction in sulfur dioxide (SO_2) emissions through a tradable permit program. The CAA also included a 2 million ton reduction in nitrogen dioxide.

The 1990 CAA was the first implementation of tradable permits in the United States, which was a substantial departure from previous command-and-control approaches. As discussed in chapter 7, tradable permits allow a firm to emit a limited amount of pollution. The permit can be used, saved, or sold to another party. At the first annual auction of permits in March of 1993, bidders paid from $122 to $450 for each of 150,000 one-ton permits. Northeast Utilities in Connecticut donated 10,000 of its permits to the American Lung Association, which then retired the permits.

Results from the innovative policy are positive. The market incentive approach, as expected, has allowed greater flexibility for firms and substantial savings for the nation. The annual emissions of SO_2 have been halved at a cost of a third to a half as much as the cost would have been using the command-and-control approach. This amounts to a saving of $1 to $2 billion annually. Many firms have met SO_2 targets by switching to low-sulfur coal or developing new fuel-blending techniques. Railroad deregulation also created cost savings, as lower coal shipping costs have led to lower coal prices. Because coal prices were lower, the price of a smokestack scrubber (a substitute for low sulfur coal) fell by half between 1990 and 1995.[7]

The tradable permit program has been successful both environmentally and economically. Additionally, this major experiment with a new policy approach provides valuable data that will improve future policy choices. Despite the success of the CAA, costs of the regulation, which include higher electricity bills and lost jobs for coal miners, are significant.

Here Comes the Sun—Duck and Cover

Most of us have heard something about the holes in the ozone layer. The ozone layer acts as a stratospheric global sunscreen that protects us from being hit with too much ultraviolet radiation from the sun. Stratospheric ozone should not be confused with ozone in the troposphere, which is the atmosphere closest to the earth. Tropospheric ozone is harmful to humans, animal, and plants. Ozone is super in the stratosphere and terrible in the troposphere. The "super" ozone absorbs about 99% of the sun's harmful incoming ultraviolet radiation, preventing it from reaching the earth's surface.

Chlorofluorocarbons (CFCs), invented in the 1940s, are very useful as refrigerants, propellants in spray cans, and solvents to clean machine parts. Unfortunately, they also deplete the ozone layer. As CFCs deplete the ozone layer, humans suffer worse sunburns, more cataracts, and more skin cancers. The National Academy of Sciences estimates that for every 1% decline in the ozone layer we will suffer an additional 10,000 cases of skin cancer each year. Also, the increased ultraviolet radiation damages plants, perhaps even reducing agriculture yield. Phytoplankton, the foundation of the oceanic food web, is also adversely affected. We really don't know the full extent of damage from CFCs.

CFCs, which cause most of the damage to the ozone layer, act as a catalyst that converts ozone to oxygen. Poof, it's gone. Because CFCs are not consumed in the chemical process, they continue to damage the ozone layer for decades. Let's pull out our bag of policy options to decide how best to stop the depletion of the ozone layer. When evidence of ozone depletion began to surface in the 1970s, various incentives such as permits, emission taxes, and deposit-refund were proposed. However, because inexpensive, good substitutes are available for CFCs, and the damage is high even at low levels of CFCs, this may well be an example where command-and-control works best.

Just such a policy was implemented in 1977. The United States banned the use of CFCs as a propellant. Ozone depletion is the result of global contributions, however, and unilateral actions are ineffective. In 1988, 24 countries signed the Montreal Protocol, which banned the emission of CFCs in developed countries by 2000 and developing countries by 2010. The agreement has worked well. Although a black market for CFCs exists, a complete phase-out of CFCs is on schedule.

Summary

Regional and global pollution problems are difficult to solve, primarily because solutions require cooperation among many nations. The world's oceans and air are common pool resources, owned by all of us and yet no person in particular. From the beginning of human civilization, we have deposited waste into the air and water without regard to the effects on others. With the growth in population and production, we have now reached a point where such behavior is very costly.

The environmental issues discussed in this chapter could have major consequences for future generations. The question is what should we do about it? First, scientists must make efforts to ascertain the facts as to the causes and effects of pollutants and inform us. Second, any effort if it is to be successful, requires coordinated efforts of all nations. We must choose efficient as well as equitable policies. Generally, the most efficient way to deal with global problems is through market-based policies. Cooperative approaches using taxes and emission permits can reduce pollution to acceptable levels at the lowest cost to society.

Chapter 9

∾∾

A Worrisome Thing:
The Environment and Economic Growth

> It remains to be seen whether this power [reproduction] canbe checked and its effects kept equal to the means of subsistence, without vice or misery.
>
> —Thomas Malthus

Twentieth century humans face a cruel dilemma. On the one hand, we urgently need to increase the output of goods and services referred to as economic growth and measured by Gross Domestic Product (GDP). Increasing GDP, which is the dollar value of a nations yearly output of goods and services, is especially important for the more than one billion people who live in poverty. Yet, on the other hand, growth in output of goods and services (i.e., GDP) consumes world resources (some that are irreplaceable), disfigures the landscape, creates health problems, and in general lowers environmental quality of life. What's the prognosis? Acrimonious debates spring from this dilemma. Let's try to clarify the issues and gain a better perspective on how we might deal with the dilemma. Along the way we consider issues of sustainable growth, GDP as a measure of well-being, and the effect of trade on the environment.

So Many People

Thomas Malthus in his 1798 *Essay on the Principle of Population* worried that population growth would surpass food supplies. Malthus concluded that pestilence, war, and hunger would continually bedevil humans. In recent decades many still voice concerns that we are stretching the carrying capacity of the planet earth beyond its capabilities. They call for limits to economic growth because of concern regarding its impact on the environment: too many people using too many resources creating too much waste.

Malthus' predictions that society would not be able to produce enough food to meet the basic needs of the population never materialized.[1] Malthus failed to anticipate the technological advances that would lead to increased food production. Since 1950, the green revolution has dramatically increased the food yield per acre. High-yield agriculture also helps to protect biodiversity because more food is grown on less land. Unfortunately, the heavy use of pesticides, herbicides, and fertilizers to increase yields causes serious environmental damage.

While Malthus' dismal predictions have not come true, humans have proliferated, especially in the past century. World population doubled between 1930 and 1975, increasing from 2 to 4 billion. From 1975 to 2000 population rose another 50% to 6 billion. Population has been doubling every 41 years. In order to keep the standard of living at current levels, we must also double the output of goods and services every 41 years. Most people, however, are not just content to maintain living standards. They want higher standards of living, especially in the poorer countries of the world. In fact, some countries must more than double output every 41 years in order to keep standards of living level since their population growth is greater than the average. For countries such as Yemen, Ethiopia, Angola, and Niger, population is projected to double between 1995 and 2015. That is twice as fast as the average country.

Some healthy signs, however, have surfaced. In recent years the average rate of population growth has declined everywhere except Africa. The total fertility rate (an estimate of the average number of children a woman will have during childbearing years) has dropped from 5 children to 3.1 children in the last four decades. The rate has decreased from 2.8 to 1.7 children in developed countries, and from 6.2 to 3.5 children in less developed nations. Projections are that population growth in developed nations will be negative by the year 2030. The United Nations predicts that world population will stabilize within the next century at just over 11 billion people. While that is still a lot of people looking for parking spaces, population growth appears to be stabilizing. Why?

While population growth drives much of the effort to increase economic growth, at some point economic growth tends to slow population expansion. According to the "theory of demographic transition," as nations develop, they reach a point where birth rates begin to fall. Certainly this has been the case in the developed countries in Western Europe, as well as in North America and Japan. Higher-income countries generally have lower population growth rates.

Many elements affect family size, including economic, cultural, social, and religious factors. Much of the slowdown in population growth is the result of changing parental preferences and modern birth control methods that allow couples around the world to control family size. Economic growth, which moves an agrarian society towards an industrialized and urbanized society, affects family size choice. In poor agrarian nations, parents are dependent in their old age on children for support. Economic growth leads to better public social systems (for example, social security programs) and consequently a decreased need for a large number of children.

Parents benefit in many ways by having children, but children also require time and household resources. As the opportunity cost of having children increases, people choose to have fewer children. Costs of education, food, and housing increase with urbanization. Also, in agrarian systems children are valuable labor to care for crops and livestock. As economies become industrialized, an educated, skilled workforce becomes more important. As the investment in an individual child's education increases, parents choose to have fewer children.

Government policies can also help control population growth. China has taken drastic action to control population growth, although many feel that their program is overly intrusive and coercive. In China, having more than one child usually requires the permission of the state. Less drastic government policies can also be effective. Providing old-age security and employment opportunities that equalize income distribution help.

Policies that encourage equal treatment of women lead to less population growth. Evidence shows that women with a good education and desirable employment opportunities feel the cost of having children through lost income. Consequently, better opportunities, which are more likely with economic growth, encourage women to have fewer children.

If population declines, one would expect per capita income to rise followed by more investment in health, education, and environmental quality. This appears to have been the case in South Korea, Taiwan, Thailand, and Singapore with Malaysia and Indonesia close behind.[2] If birth rates continue to decline, higher economic growth rates will be less important.

Others, who expect technological improvements to increase output and also help protect the environment, are less alarmed about population growth. Yet, still others worry that even if we are able to increase output enough to keep up with population growth, do we want to live in a world that is so crowded?

To make matters worse, the world's output is not evenly divided. Per capita GDP in 1995 varied from $26,721 for Switzerland to $171 for Sierra Leone. In that same year average per capita GDP for the developing countries (that is, the poorer ones) was $867, while the average per capita GDP for the industrial countries (the richer ones) was $12,764, a startling difference.[3] Pressure from the poorer countries and the not-so-poor countries for more economic growth and higher standards of living is universal.

While more population adds to the workforce and presumably the nation's output, it often leads to increased poverty and income inequality. Most of the poorer countries cannot generate jobs and income fast enough to keep up with the population growth, which causes greater pressure for even higher levels of growth. Furthermore, poorer families tend to have larger families and invest less in education, saving, and health, further exacerbating income inequality.

All of us want more income and higher standards of living. In the poorer countries it is a matter of life and death. In the richer countries it is simply improving the quality of life above levels that are already comfortable. This is why economic growth receives such widespread support. It is sought with something close to religious fervor. Rarely is economic growth policy questioned. Jobs, jobs, jobs, more industrial plants, roads, schools, houses, and shopping centers. What is and will be the impact of economic growth on our resources and environmental quality?

Development and the Environment

Many believe that economic growth causes greater environmental degradation. Economic growth, unless controlled, may cause environmental degradation because growing economies crave more goods, use more resources, and emit more pollutants. Too often growth causes polluted air and water, noisy and congested streets, and dwindling forests and biodiversity.

Developing nations currently create about 30% of the world's carbon dioxide emissions, the major cause of global warming. If current trends continue, developing nations will produce 50% of the world's carbon dioxide in the next couple of decades. Such projections have caused many, especially environmentalists, to view economic growth as the main problem.

Advocates of this position propose that we practice "sustainable development," although the meaning of the concept is ambiguous. According to the 1987 study by the World Commission on Environment and Development, sustainable development "meets the needs of the present without compromising the ability of future generations to meet their own needs." This definition suggests that while we should protect the environment for future generations, we should not ignore the needs of people today.

Sustainable development suggests that economic growth can occur over the long term, if controlled. Adherents to this thesis recognize an obligation to future generations, economically and environmentally. However, the guidelines for sustainable growth are not specific. For instance, saving a particular species is not required in order to follow a sustainable growth rule. Investment in knowledge and capital may be as valuable as protecting the environment for the well-being of future generations.

An argument can be made that economic growth is vital if we are to protect the environment. Evidence indicates that although some types of pollution initially increase as developing nations grow, after a time, environmental quality improves.[4] Countries often damage the environment in generating income to meet basic needs. Concern over the environment comes only after one has a full belly. Indeed, the most serious environmental problem in less developed nations is often unsafe drinking water.

As we have discussed, habitat protection and pollution control are not free, so with higher incomes people are in a better financial position to pay for environmental amenities. Furthermore, the technology required to ameliorate environmental problems is expensive. High economic growth rates make it easier to make the financial investment. Also, as incomes rise so does leisure, which allows greater appreciation of the environment. Consequently, the willingness to pay for environmental protection as incomes rises improves. Finally, economic growth creates conditions that encourage families to limit their size.

The environment often suffers when people experience difficult economic times. A case in point is Indonesia. Although environmental protection has been a problem in In-

donesia, in recent years a growing middle class has worked
to protect the country's unique biodiversity. Yet, when the
Indonesian economy experienced a serious recession in
1998, which brought annual inflation rates of 80% and a
tripling of the poverty rate in some areas, environmental
concern decreased. Indonesians increased clear-cutting of
ancient hardwoods, fished coral reefs with dynamite, and
sold rare species such as macaques for consumption. The
rarest species sold for little more than the most common
wild-pig meat. Indonesians increasingly harvested wildlife,
including many species of plants and animals threatened
with extinction.[5] This is especially troubling because Indonesia is home to more plant and animal species than any
country in the world, except for Brazil. Similarly, the Brazilians' slash-and-burn methods, aimed at increasing food and
output, have significantly reduced the Amazon rain forest.
Because many species exist only in Indonesia and Brazil,
we are witnessing an irreversible tragedy of the commons.

Developing nations have some of the world's most valuable biodiversity and environmental amenities, yet they
destroy many unique environments in their quest for economic development. Of course, developed nations did the
same as they progressed. Although some measures such as
better-defined property rights can help protect biodiversity,
the real hope may lie in a prosperous economy.

In Honduras, the severe hardship created by 1998 Hurricane Mitch illustrated the link between population,
poverty, and environmental damage. Honduras has the
highest population growth and the highest deforestation
rate in Central America. Deforestation causes soil erosion,
which makes flooding from heavy rains much worse. Brazil,
faced with pressure from its disproportionately large group
of low-income citizens, has been pressing ahead in deforestation efforts in the Amazon in an attempt to grow more food
and generate income, even in the face of world opposition.

If economic growth is important for environmental
quality, the reverse may also be true. Environmental damage can slow economic growth and detract from economic
well-being. When a country like Honduras creates defor-

estation, which leads to soil erosion, farming, fisheries, and future forest production all suffer. Poor environmental quality often leads to more disease, such as malaria, which decreases worker productivity.

In less developed nations, property rights tend to be poorly defined. As discussed earlier in Chapter 3, when access to a resource is not controlled, users will overuse resources, as is often the case with tropical forests. Property rights are often poorly defined for renewable resources such as water, air, fish, forests, and biodiversity. On the other hand, because property rights are well defined for most nonrenewable resources, such as minerals, higher prices encourage conservation and substitution, and more efficient use.

Greater damage to the environment may result when a nation does not have well-defined property rights. Without well-defined property rights, the long-term value of an asset is ignored. A property owner will treat his or her property as a long-term asset and not misuse it because he or she will weigh future profits against current profits. As a resource becomes scarcer and value increases, a private owner has an incentive to protect the resource, while commonly-owned property with open access will be depleted more rapidly. If better-defined property rights coincide with economic growth, one would expect better environmental protection also.

What Does GDP Measure?

For many, the debate over economic growth goes on as if we all are in agreement on what economic growth is. Usually, economic growth is measured in terms of the rate at which GDP increases. GDP is a monetary measure of an economy's output, but it is not necessarily a good indicator of economic well-being. And it's not meant to be.

Here's a short list of some of the things missed by GDP. Because only products sold through the market are counted, we sometimes ignore environmental quality, red cockaded woodpeckers, and leisure. Even things that are made for personal use, such as food grown in a garden, are not counted, and goods and services associated with the "underground economy" are left out of the count.

Economic "bads" such as pollution control equipment, police protection, and medical facilities to deal with health problems caused by pollution, are not subtracted, although as these costs increase we are worse off. Replacement of homes and other possessions that are destroyed by natural disasters such as hurricanes and tornadoes are added to GDP. Similarly, the production of cleaning materials and the salaries paid to clean up workers from the Exxon *Valdez* oil spill were added to GDP.

As human-created capital wears out (machinery), the depreciation value is subtracted from GDP to get Net National Product. GDP does not subtract the natural resources that are depleted. A nation could be ripping through the natural resource base and showing strong economic growth, but not sustainable growth. This may be a very serious problem in developing nations where economic growth policies get such high priority. A 1989 study showed that when depreciation of Indonesian forests, petroleum reserves, and soil assets were included in GDP calculation, growth rates fell significantly below conventional figures.[6]

Nordhaus and Tobin attempt to remedy these deficiencies by adding in those things left out and subtracting the economic bads in their Measure of Economic Welfare calculation. Some suggest incorporating sustainability into a measure of growth. Daly and Cobb have proposed an Index of Sustainable Economic Welfare (ISEW). The ISEW measures personal consumption and adjusts for the degree of inequality in income distribution, depletion of natural capital, pollution costs, and increases in foreign debt, among other factors.[7]

GDP, however, does include all goods and services that are environmental in nature. For example, smokestack scrubbers, catalytic converters, and new sewage treatment plants are included in GDP. So in this sense, economic growth (that is, a rise in GDP) is compatible with a rise in environmental quality. Therefore, rising demand for environmental quality can lead to more investment in environmental protection, higher GDP, and higher environmental standards. In the United States we have experienced both rising GDP and higher levels of environmental quality.

Trade and the Environment

Generally, economists favor free trade between nations because consumers enjoy lower prices and greater variety of goods and services. On balance, all nations benefit from more efficient production. Despite the unquestionable economic gains from free trade, there are those, such as displaced textile workers in the United States, who lose. We all remember Ross Perot's "great sucking sound" argument in the debate over the North American Free Trade Agreement (NAFTA). However, for this book we will avoid extensive treatment of these concerns and focus instead on what effect, if any, free trade has on the environment.

Some are concerned that free trade will encourage industries to move to countries with less stringent environmental regulation. If true, local areas may suffer from increased pollution in exchange for more income and jobs. Some were concerned that the NAFTA would cause U.S. industries to flee to Mexico in order to take advantage of the less strict environmental regulations. However, studies offer little evidence that companies flee to "pollution havens." This may in part be due to the fact that pollution-control costs generally are a small proportion of overall production costs. Also, Mexican law requires U.S. firms operating in Mexico to meet U.S. regulations. Some worry that companies in the United States will battle for less strict environmental regulation in order to compete with nations with less environmental restrictions.

Others worry that international groups such as the World Trade Organization (WTO) will encourage actions that will damage the environment. Most nations belong to the WTO, which establishes procedures that define "fair trade practices." The United States could not require Mexico to produce "dolphin safe" tuna, although U.S. producers did produce tuna that was "dolphin safe." According to the WTO this would be unfair discrimination. Although such "discrimination" may be justified, companies may claim an interest in protecting the environment, when instead they are concerned with limiting competition. If U.S. consumers demand protection for dolphins, and are willing to pay higher prices for this protection, companies will certainly comply.

Evidence so far does not seem to support the dire predictions of environmental damage that some thought would result from NAFTA and other similar agreements. Proponents of free trade argue that the economic gains from trade will reduce poverty and slow population growth. This will allow investment in water and air quality improvement, as well as health care and education. The economic growth will enable nations to pay for environmental protection and new technology. Free trade will increase productivity and economic efficiency.

Trade between nations may also provide a basis for agreement on important environmental policies that require international cooperation. If free trade leads to economic growth, and unacceptable environmental damage results, then some kind of government involvement may be needed.

Protecting the environment is further complicated because countries are mutually interdependent in ways never experienced before. Environmentally-damaging activities may be curtailed in one nation only to be transferred to another nation. The end result may be more damage than if the original activity had continued. For example, as timber harvests were reduced in the U.S. West (partly because of concerns over the spotted owl), other regions, including the U.S. South, Latin America, Russia, and Asia increased timber harvests. Some of the areas are in old-growth forests.[8] When the logging takes place in old-growth tropical forests, environmental damage could be high, especially to biodiversity. Perhaps the best way to protect the greatest amount of the environment is to recognize regions where damage is most severe and devise incentives that address problems in those areas. In today's global business environment we must realize that sometimes doing "good" at the local level can have "bad" results globally.

Summary

Environmental protection, population growth, and economic growth are linked. Some evidence exists that population growth retards economic growth because big families are usually poor families who have little to invest in education, health, and saving. But whether this theory is true or not, economic growth can lead to reduced population growth, higher living standards, and increased environmental protection. Yet, we must recognize that economic growth also can create more pollution and resource use, which can damage the environment. Which is it? Is economic growth a good thing or a bad thing? As usual, it is neither black nor white. Policies that encourage sustainable development may be the key.

If we can create enough environmental protection in the early stages of development, once a country's standard of living reaches some acceptable level, demands for environmental amenities tend to automatically increase. Lower population growth rates and greater demands for a higher quality of life will support the push for environmental protection. This process can be reinforced with better-defined and protected property rights, and government policies compatible with free markets.

International cooperation may be necessary in order to solve some of the more difficult environmental problems, such as global warming, species loss, and depletion of ocean fisheries. A better understanding and promotion of international relationships is imperative as we seek solutions to these problems.

Chapter 10

‿‿

Conclusion:
I'm Beginning to See the Light

Man is but a reed, the weakest in nature, but he is a thinking reed.

—Pascal, *Thoughts*, ch. ii, 10

By most criteria humankind has enjoyed tremendous success over the years, especially in the Twentieth century. Our species has proliferated. We've multiplied our numbers from 1 to 6 billion in the Twentieth century alone. Infant mortality has dropped from 170 per 1,000 in 1950 to less than 60 today, and life expectancy has increased from 30 to 66 years. World per capita income continues to rise, resulting in higher standards of living, improved health, higher life expectancy rates, and greater economic security.

But all these gains in human welfare have come with a price tag attached. One of the prices we have paid and continue to pay is in the form of environmental deterioration. We are draining aquifers, depleting fisheries, denuding forests, and eliminating biodiversity. We are polluting the water, air, and land locally, regionally, and globally.

As we've become more aware of the severity of environmental problems in the final decades of this century, we've begun to weigh the cost of economic progress and growing population numbers, question the merits of past actions, and propose policies based on assessments of benefits and costs. Today, most nations have some type of regulatory agency that attempts to improve environmental quality. World-wide discussions and agreements have materialized, and cooperative efforts (such as the Kyoto accord) are under way to address global problems such as ozone depletion and global warming. We believe economists have a lot to offer in shaping the debate over the extent of the problem and policy options that might be devised and implemented.

Green Religion

According to a 1998 World Wildlife Fund survey, people are concerned about the environment, but "greens" fanaticism, for many, turns concern into apathy. If people are continually bombarded with warnings of how difficult it is to solve environmental problems they become frustrated. In fact, a 1999 review of public opinion polls indicates Americans are discouraged over the difficulty of solving environmental problems and are beginning to lose interest. We believe a more reasoned and practical approach to the problem is called for.

Environmentalists are sometimes a lot like clergymen: both groups preach that some specific acts are wrong and sinful, and the solution is in recognizing this fact and changing human behavior. Stealing is wrong. It is a violation of one of the 10 Commandments handed down to Moses by God. The remedy for a thief is to confess the sin and go thy way and sin no more.

Many environmentalists follow a similar path. Barry Lopez writes: "But I ask myself, where is the man or woman, standing before lifeless porpoises strangled and bloated in a beachcast drift net, or standing on farmland ankle deep in soil gone to flour dust, or flying over the Cascade Mountains and seeing the clearcuts stretching for forty miles, the sunbaked earth, the steams running with mud, who does not want to say, 'Forgive me, thou bleeding earth, that I am meek and gentle with these butchers?'"[1]

Lopez goes on to say "What we face is a crisis of culture, a crisis of character." And "It is not a crisis of policy or a law or of administration. We cannot turn to institutions, to environmental groups, or to government. We have a monumental adjustment to make. We must turn to each other, and sense that this is possible."[2]

Many feel that religion is the only answer. "Only a new religion of nature, similar but even more powerful than the animal rights movement, can create the political momentum required to overcome the greed that gives rise to discord and strife and the anthropocentrism that underlies the intentional abuse of nature."[3]

It is certainly true that awareness of human's impact on the ecosystem is absolutely necessary as a prerequisite for dealing with environmental problems, and all of us are deeply indebted to environmentalists such as Carson, Lopez, and Wilson for bringing this awareness to the table. But, while recognition of the dimensions of the environmental problem is essential, that alone is insufficient in formulating solutions, and here is where the social scientists must join the dialog. Recognition and confession of sin is one thing and may even be good for the soul, but changing one's lifestyle from sin to purity is quite another.

Some individuals do repent and change their sinful behavior. Most do not. Some individuals realize the importance of preserving streams and woodlands and follow through by planting trees and avoiding actions that pollute the air and water. Most do not, especially when incentives drive us in the opposite direction. How do we change an entire nation's or region's way of life? How do we go from individual cases to whole populations?

The Value of Knowing Some Economics

There are natural forces beyond our control that dramatically alter the environment—El Niños, hurricanes, tsunamis, volcanoes, earthquakes, sea level rise, plate tectonics. Humankind dramatically alters the environment by contributing to ozone depletion, acid rain, global warming, and species extinction. Contrary to most natural forces, human behavior can be changed, not so much by preaching but by using economic incentives to cause voluntary changes in behavior.

Throughout this book we have tried to illustrate the value of economic principles in our efforts to solve environmental problems. Those who wish to protect the environment will do well to understand some economics. Here's a summary of a few of the things we think are important.

We must make choices about how to use scarce resources. We aren't provided with any "free lunches." The market system is the best method for satisfying societal wants and needs. But nobody, absolutely nobody, thinks the market system is perfect. Simply put; it is the best of available alternatives in much the same way that democracy, despite its weaknesses, is the best of available political systems.

Unfortunately, sometimes unfettered markets lead to the misuse of the environment. Economics helps us to understand why we damage the environment. Usually the problem is that property rights are poorly defined and enforced. Resources such as air and water are owned by everyone; consequently, no one feels compelled to protect them. When you offer something for "free," individuals will overuse it. Why pay to treat wastewater when you can dump it free of charge into a passing stream? Why filter out air contaminants from electronic blast furnaces when they can be freely sent up a smokestack into the atmosphere. Given the competitive nature of markets, it is too much to expect that a firm fighting for its economic survival will voluntarily impose higher costs on itself in order to keep the water and air pure. It is much easier to pass the costs onto the rest of us. It is not a question of what "ought to be" but a question of "what is."

A valuable lesson we should get from economic analysis is that generally the "best" level of pollution is not zero. Generally, creating pollution is not considered by most of us to be an immoral act. Pollution is a residual of the production process that provides the goods and services that we want and need. However, because the market system ordinarily does not punish polluters, some government intervention may be necessary. Nobody thinks such government intervention will have perfect outcomes either. So, to enact effective and efficient policies, agencies must have information about the costs and benefits of their actions, and must enact policies that intermesh and harmonize with market forces.

Economics also provides valuable information about the best ways to limit environmental damage. The solution is to encourage individuals, owners of firms, and governments to take responsibility for the costs they impose on others. Policies that create better-defined property rights will internalize costs, and make the owners better stewards of the resources they control because their self-interest is harmed if they don't.

A better understanding of economic theory can lead to improvement in environmental policy. Better policy can harness the power of self-interest and market incentives to correct environmental problems at the least cost to society. Market incentives can create results that meet moral needs beyond simply efficiency. Although solutions are not always easily implemented (biodiversity loss will require major policy change, for example), incentives can be altered to improve all environmental problems. But all environmental amenities come at some price. Economics offers better possibilities for environmental success than an ecological awakening, ala a religious revival.

Over the past three decades, environmental policy has improved environmental quality. However, we may have picked the "low-hanging fruit," and additional environmental protection will likely become increasingly more expensive. We will need to implement future policies with increased awareness of cost-effectiveness. Economics provides valuable information on the benefits and costs of the choices that we must make. Although measuring benefits and costs is often difficult and controversial, the process is invaluable. Society may even choose to ignore the results of such assessments when following a moral imperative, such as protecting species regardless of cost. But, we still should not ignore the costs of our actions.

One thing is clear; policy should be well crafted and incremental. As the old carpenter adage says, "Measure twice and cut once." Policy should also be flexible so that we can change directions cheaply and quickly when we detect inappropriate policy initiatives.

One of the troubling things about altering human behavior in ways that preserve the environment, as we know it, is that we have only a glimpse of how the future will be transformed by new technologies. The information age is catapulting us into an unknown future. As Jeremy Rifkin points out, It is the dawn of the Age of Biotechnology with genetically engineered plants and animals, wonder drugs and all the rest. Rifkin queries ". . . will the mass release of thousands of genetically engineered life forms into the environment cause catastrophic genetic pollution and irreversible damage to the biosphere?" and " At what cost?"[4] About such things we can only theorize.

However, looking backward is not the answer. In 1811, the Luddites, who were disgruntled British workers rebelling against new labor-saving technology in the textile industry, smashed machinery in a vain attempt to halt the industrial revolution. Following a mass trial and hanging of the ressurectionists in 1813, the short-lived revolt ended. We still use the term Luddites today to indicate a reaction against technological change. But it is unlikely that technological advances will be halted, nor should they be. For if we wish to create positive change for the environment, we must enact laws and instigate programs that utilize the latest technology in maintaining and improving environmental standards.

The Importance of Communicating Across Disciplines

We reiterate and echo E. O. Wilson's call for interdisciplinary work when dealing with environmental concerns. A joint understanding of scientific relationships and economic principles is necessary for the best solutions to our problems. A proper policy mix requires no less.

Economics and ecology share the Greek *oikos*, which means "house" or "place to live." Ecologists study the relationships between organisms and their homes. Economists study the choices humans make as they attempt to provide for their well-being. The two disciplines are closely linked, but all too often the disciplines ignore the insights and expertise of the other. "What we have here is a failure to communicate," as Strother Martin drawled in *Cool Hand Luke*.

We expect that many environmentalists, ecologists, and economists can agree on many issues. First, markets are not perfect. For example, product price is not always a good indicator of production cost. Second, governments are not perfect. For example, the command-and-control approach to environmental control, traditionally favored by government, is usually much more costly than alternatives. Third, the value of nonmarket goods is difficult to determine. For instance, what is a beautiful sunset worth? Fourth, markets do some things very well. Markets mitigate general resource scarcity and maximize consumer welfare levels. Fifth, government subsidies are costly and environmentally destructive. For instance, farm subsidies cause excessive use of pesticides that kill fish and pollute streams and lakes. Sixth, healthy economic systems depend on a healthy environment. For example, deforestation will dampen future farm, fishery, and forestry production.

Some differences between economists and environmentalists still exist. For example, some doubt the efficacy of market incentives for solving pollution problems. However, many including Ehrlich, World Watch Institute, and Dave Foreman, founder of EarthFirst, have expressed positive statements about market incentives.

We have unique environmental problems to solve today. Because outcomes from societal actions such as species loss, global warming, and ozone depletion may be irreversible, we need to act now. However, there is cause for optimism. We can solve many of the problems if we recognize the causes that create the problems and the forces that move individuals towards the proper actions. Although economics may not provide sufficient analysis to solve all the problems, certainly economics is integral to most solutions as we attempt to choose the best solutions.

For Art and the Environment

Thirty thousand years ago early humans created cave paintings at Lascaux in Southern France. We aren't sure what message the early artists were trying to convey, although we suspect that they were trying to understand and control forces that determined their survival. Perhaps the hunting scenes were meant to be hunting magic, or they may have been a hunting tutorial demonstrating the surest method for a kill. Whatever the intent of the artists, these were a people dependent on a healthy environment for survival.

A thousand years ago in the Southwestern United States the Anasazi also depended on a healthy environment for survival. Some Anasazi art that remains (pictographs and petroglyphs that were painted and carved onto cliffs), most likely have astronomical significance. The art illustrates the importance of the seasons' rhythms for survival, and probably indicate concerns about spiritual needs as well as for rain and wild game. The industrious Anasazi understanding of nature's rhythms allowed them to maintain a fragile existence in an arid environment for centuries. Evidence suggests that the Anasazi abruptly abandoned Chaco Canyon after they depleted the resources and damaged the environment to the point that they no longer could survive.

Today, because of advancements in knowledge and technology, we can satisfy basic needs more efficiently than our ancestors could. Consequently, we have more time to enjoy art that can help us make order from the clutter of daily existence. Artists help us understand the human condition and the forces that determine our survival. We recognize that the quality of life would be diminished without the arts, so consequently we encourage artistic expression. However, programs like the Dutch art subsidy that encouraged art suitable for recycling, are incorrectly designed. In this same vein, we must design and initiate environmental policies that avoid the Dutch dilemma but instead lead to desired environmental results.

Proper actions can be undertaken only when we understand the interaction of environmental and economic forces. We are after all, still dependent on the natural world for our survival. Unlike the Anasazi, we don't have the option of simply moving on if we ruin the only environment that we have.

Notes

Chapter 1

1. E. O. Wilson, *Consilience*, p. 195.

2. Timothy Ryback, "The Dutch Dilemma: Is It Art? Is It Trash? Or Is It Both?", pp. 210–214.

3. E. O. Wilson, ibid., pp. 280–286.

4. Bert Lindler, "Making Economics Less Dismal," p. 10.

5. Randey Meiners and Bruce Yandle, The Common Law: How it Protects the Environment, p. 3.

6. Peter Waldman, "Desperate Indonesians Devour Country's Trove of Endangered Species, p. 1.

7. Paul Portney, "Counting the Cost," p. 15.

8. GDP is the dollar value of real final goods and services produced in the United States over the course of a year.

9. Aldo Leopold, *A Sand County Almanac*, p. 28.

10. Mitch Friedman, "Earth in the Balance Sheet," p. 6.

11. Wallace Kaufman, *No Turning Back*, p. 53.

12. Walter Williams, All It Takes Is Guts.

13. Lester Milbrath, *Learning to Think Environmentally*, p. xii.

14. Robert Heilbroner, *The Making of Economic Society*, pp. 42–46.

Chapter 2

1. B. G. DeSylva, Lew Brown, Roy Henderson.

2. Lester Brown, et al., *State of the World 1998*, p. 44.

3. *The Appalachian Voice,* letter to the editor, p. 2.

4. Paul and Anne Ehrlich, *Betrayal of Science and Reason*, p. 92.

5. Robert Mundell, *Man and Economics*, p. 1.

6. Stacy Kravetz, "Dry Cleaner's New Wrinkle: Going Green," p. B1.

7. James Rinehart and Jackson F. Lee, *"The Optimum Level of Ignorance: Marginal Analysis in Education,"* pp. 30–31.

8. Although China's population control policy has been successful, the coercive nature of the program raises concerns. We consider other measures that can contribute to population control in chapter 8.

9. Bob Davis, "Think Big," p. R14.

10. Robert Heilbroner, *The Making of Economic Society*, pp. 12–13.

Chapter 3

1. Jared Diamond, "The Golden Age that Never Was," p. 79.

2. Paul and Anne Ehrlich, *Betrayal of Science and Reason*, p. 186.

3. Wendell Berry quoted in Wallace Kaufman, *No Turning Back*, p. 51.

4. Feshbach and Friendly, *Ecocide in the USSR.*

5. Al Gore, *Earth in the Balance*, p. 20.

6. David Orr, *Earth in Mind*, p. 168.

7. John Kenneth Galbraith, *The Affluent Society.*

8. R. Kerry Turner, David Pearce, and Ian Bateman, *Environmental Economics*, p. 311.

9. In chapter 6 we discuss the recently introduced "safe harbor" program, which is a possible remedy for this problem.

10. Al Gore, ibid., p. 3.

11. Elinor Ostrom, *Governing the Commons*, p. 61.

12. James Kahn, *Economic Approach to Environmental and Natural Resources*, p. 377.

13. May/June 1998 Audubon Mag. John Dillon, "Why Birds Hate Seinfeld," p. 16.

14. Lester Milbrath, *Learning to Think Environmentally*, p. 78.

15. David Bush, et al., *Living by the Rules of the Sea*, pp. 148–149.

16. National Wildlife Foundation, "Higher Ground," pp. 23–25

17. Thomas Sowell, "Disaster Aid," p. 11A.

18. Terry Anderson, "Water Options for the Blue Planet," p. 277.

19. Sandra Postel, "Increasing Water Efficiency," p. 57.

20. Terry Anderson, ibid., p. 280.

21. William Martin, et al., *Saving Water in A Desert City*, pp. 109–112.

22. David Roodman, *Natural Wealth of Nations*, p. 35.

Chapter 4

1. E. O. Wilson, *On Human Nature*, p. 107.

2. Aldo Leopold, *A Sand County Almanac*, p. 26.

3. John Duffield and David Patterson, "Field Testing Existence Values: An Instream Flow Trust Fund for Monitoring Rivers."

4. Jonathan Rubin, et al., "A Benefit-Cost Analysis of the Northern Spotted Owl," pp. 25–30.

5. National Oceanographic and Atmospheric Administration (report), 58 FR 4602, January 15, 1993.

6. Geoffrey Heal, *Nature and the Marketplace*, pp. 49–52.

7. *The State* newspaper, "Environmentalists Sue Forestry Service," p. 925.

8. Stephen Kellert, *The Value of Life*, p. 165.

9. Ibid., p. 177.

10. John Krutilla and Anthony Fisher, *The Economics of Natural Environments*, pp. 125–141.

Chapter 5

1. Photographers' Cheesecake: Line a baking tin with pastry. Bake at 375° for 10 minutes. Melt 1 stick of butter. Stir in 4 oz. of sugar and yolks of 3 eggs. Add a pinch of nutmeg, a pinch of salt, and the juice of 1 lemon. Stir all ingredients well. Pour mixture into pastry tin and bake at 375° for 30 minutes. The top should be a beautiful gold/bronze. Pretty as a picture. (You're on your own for the whites.) Heinz Henisch, *The Photographic Experience*, p. 57.

2. Jeff Bailey, "Curbside Recycling Comforts the Soul but Benefits are Scant," p. 1.

3. Don Fullerton and Thomas Kinnaman, "Household's Responses to Pricing Garbage by the Bag," pp. 971–984.

4. Curiously, a major impetus for the formation of Yellowstone came from the owners of the Northern Pacific Railroad, who hoped to receive revenue from tourists traveling the Park.

5. John Hartwick and Nancy Olewiler, *The Economics of Natural Resource Use*, p. 173.

6. Bill Richards. "Fishermen in Alaska," p. 1.

7. James Rinehart and Jeffrey Pompe, "Entrepreneurship and Coastal Resource Management," p. 553.

8. John Krutilla, "Conservation Reconsidered," p. 195.

9. Paul Ehrlich and Anne Ehrlich, *Betrayal of Science and Reason*, p. 92.

10. Ronald Bailey, *EcoScam*, p. 76.

Chapter 6

1. E. O. Wilson, *Consilience*, p. 293.

2. Erin Schiller, "Delhi Fly and Property Rights Can Coexist," p. 1.

3. M. Bean and D. Wilcove. "Private Land Problem," pp. 1–2.

4. Aldo Leopold, Conservation Economics, p. 202.

5. Lee Ann Welch, "Property Rights Conflicts Under the Endangered Species Act: Protection of the Red-Cockaded Woodpecker," pp. 173–175.

6. J. Pompe and J. Rinehart. *The Lucas Case and the Conflict over Property Rights.*

7. Jeffrey Pompe and Travis Knowles, The Safe Harbor Program for Red-Cockaded Woodpeckers in South Carolina, pp. 10–12.

8. Amy Ando, "Ecosystems, Interest Groups, and the ESA," p. 8.

9. Roger Sedjo and R. David Simpson, Property Rights Contracting and the Commercialization of Biodiversity, p. 175.

10. Phillip Davis, "Guyana," July 12, 1998.

11. R. David Simpson, et al., Valuing Biodiversity for Use in Pharmaceutical Research, pp. 170–172.

12. Jeffrey Pompe and Travis Knowles, The Safe Harbor Program for Red-Cockaded Woodpeckers in South Carolina, pp. 9–12.

13. Randall O'toole, *Fixing the Endangered Species Act.* www.teleport.com/~rst/esa.html.

14. Whit Gibbons, "Why do bootleggers make good conservationists?" http://www.uga.edu/srelherp/ecoview/eco4.htm.

Chapter 7

1. Paul Portney, "Counting the Cost," p. 36.

2. Caleb Solomen, "What Really Pollutes? Study of Refinery Proves an Eye-Opener," p. 1.

3. Jeffrey Taylor, "New Rules Harness Power of Free Markets to Curb Air Pollution," p. 1.

4. Paul Portney, "Counting the Cost."

5. John Mitchell, In the Wake of the Spill, p. 100.

6. Both the consumer and producer share in the cost of regulation. The producer is unable to force the full cost of regulation onto the consumer, because consumers will buy less at higher prices.

7. *The Post and Courier*, April 2, 1999, p. A1.

8. Bruce Yandle, "Bootleggers, Baptists, and Global Warming, p. 6.

9. Terry Anderson, *Political Environmentalism*, p. xi.

10. Frank Graham, Jr., The Audobon Ark, quoted from *EnviroCapitalists*, p. 43, Anderson and Leal.

11. *The Cousteau Almanac*, p. 586.

12. The snail darter was successfully transplanted to the nearby Hiawassee River.

13. The Spring Pond Beavers, *Wall Street Journal,* p. A18, March 30, 1998.

14. J. Clarence Davies and Jan Mazurek, "Pollution Control in the United States," pp. 123–148.

15. Paul Ehrlich, *Betrayal of Science and Reason*, p. 178.

16. Lester Brown, et al., *State of the World 1998*, p. 181.

Chapter 8

1. Jay Lehr and Diane Carol Bast, "Kyoto is Dead," pp. 13–14.

2. William Nordhaus, Dec. 18, 1998, RFF seminar.

3. We discussed the Baptists and Bootleggers analogy in chapter 7.

4. William Nordhaus, *Managing the Global Commons*, pp. 180–182.

5. Curtis Freese, *Wild Species as Commodities*, p. 41.

6. Driscoll, et al., *Acid Rain Revisited*, pp. 2–3.

7. Dallas Burtraw, Trading Emissions to Clean the Air: Exchanges Few But Savings Many, pp. 5–6.

Chapter 9

1. Although world hunger does exist, malnourishment is the result of food distribution problems. Poverty is the root cause. Continued population growth may exceed production capabilities, given the limited supply of land.

2. Richard P. Cincotta and Robert Engelman, "Economics and Rapid Change: The Influence of Population Growth," pp. 23–24.

3. United Nations, *Human Development Report*, p. 10.

4. Gene Grossman and Paul Krueger, "Economic Growth and the Environment," pp. 374–377.

5. Peter Waldman, "Desperate Indonesians Devour Country's Trove of Endangered Species," p. 1.

6. Robert Repetto, "Nature's Resources as Productive Assets," pp. 17–18.

7. Herman Daly and John Cobb, *For the Common Good*, pp. 76–77.

8. Roger Sedjo, "The Global Environmental Effects of Local Logging Cutbacks," pp. 782–784.

Chapter 10

1. Barry Lopez, *The Rediscovery of North America*, pp. 42–43.

2. Ibid., pp. 57–58.

3. Michael Soule, "Biophilia: Unanswered Question," p. 454.

4. Jeremy Rifkin, *The Biotech Century*.

Bibliography and Selected Readings

Allen, William R. *The Midnight Economist*. Sun Lakes, AZ: Thomas Horton & Daughters, 1997.

Anderson, Curt. *Economics and the Environment*. New York: National Council on Economic Education, 1996.

Anderson, Terry and Donald Leal. *EnviroCapitalists*. Lanham, MD: Rowman and Littlefield, 1997.

Anderson, Terry. "Water Options for the Blue Planet." In *The True State of the Planet*, edited by Ronald Bailey. New York, NY: The Free Press, pp. 268–294, 1995.

Anderson, Terry and P. J. Hill. "Rents from Amenity Resources: A Case Study of Yellowstone National Park." In *The Political Economy of the American West*, edited by Terry Anderson and Peter Hill, Lanhan, MD: Rowman and Littlefield, 1994.

Ando, Amy. "Ecosystems, Interest Groups, and the ESA." *Resources*, Winter 1998.

Ayres, Roy and Allen Kneese, "Production, Consumption, and Externalities," *American Economic Review* 59, 1969: 282–297.

Bailey, Jeff. "Curbside Recycling Comforts the Soul but Benefits are Scant," *Wall Street Journal* (January 19, 1995): 1.

Bailey, Ronald. *EcoScam: The False Prophesies of Ecological Apocalypse*. New York: St. Martin's Press, 1993.

———. The True State of the Planet. New York: The Free Press, 1995.

M. Bean and D. Wilcove. "Private Land Problem." *Conservation Biology* 11:1–2, 1997.

Boulding, Kenneth. "The Economics of the Coming Spaceship Earth." In *Environmental Quality in A Growing Economy*, edited by Harry Jarrett. Baltimore: Johns Hopkins University Press, 1966, pp. 3–14.

Brown, Lester, Christopher Flavin, and Hilary French. *State of the World 1998*. New York: Norton and Company, 1998.

Buchholz, Todd. *From Here to Eternity*. New York, NY: Dutton, 1995.

Burtraw, Dallas. "Trading Emissions to Clean the Air: Exchanges Few But Savings Many." *Resources* no. 122 (Winter 1996): 3–6.

Bush, D. M., O. H. Pilkey, and W. J. Neal. *Living by the Rules of the Sea*. Durham, NC: Duke Univ. Press, 1996.

Cincotta, Richard P. and Robert Engelman. "Economics and Rapid Change: The Influence of Population Growth," Occasional Paper 3, Population Action International, Oct. 1997.

Coase, Ronald. "The Problem of Social Costs." *The Journal of Law and Economics* 3:(1960) 1–44.

Cousteau, Jacques-Yves. *The Cousteau Almanac*. New York: Doubleday and Company, 1981.

Daly, Herman. "Toward a Stationary-State Economy." In *Patient Earth*, edited by J. Harte and R. Socolow. New York: Holt, Rinehart and Winston, 1971, pp. 226–244.

Daly, Herman and John Cobb. *For the Common Good*. Boston: Beacon Press, 1990.

Davies, J. Clarence and Jan Mazurek. "Pollution Control in the U.S.: Evaluation of the System." *Resources* (Winter 1998).

Davis, Bob. "Think Big." *Wall Street Journal*. January 11, p. R14, 1999.

Davis, Phillip. "Guyana," *Weekend All Things Considered*. National Public Radio, July 12, 1998.

Diamond, Jared. "The Golden Age that Never Was." *Discover* (Dec. 1988): 71–79.

Dillon, John. "Why Birds Hate Seinfeld," *Audubon Magazine* May/June 1998, p. 16.

Driscoll, C. T., G. B. Lawrence, A. J. Bulger, T. J. Butler, C. S. Cronan, C. Eager, K. F. Lambert, G. E. Likens, J. L. Stoddard, and K. C. Weathers. *Acid Rain Revisited: Advances in Scientific Understanding Since the Passage of the 1970 and 1990 Clean Air Act Amendments*. Hubard Brook Research Foundation. Science Links Publication. Vol. 1, no. 1, 2001.

Duffield, John W. and David A. Patterson. "Field Testing Existence Values: An Instream Flow Trust Fund for Montana Rivers." Paper presented at the annual meeting of the AEA. January 1991, New Orleans.

Dye, Lee. "Save the World? Maybe Later." September 3, 1998. http://more.abcnews.go.com/sections/science/DyeHard/dye71.html.

Ehrlich, Paul and Anne Ehrlich. *Betrayal of Science and Reason*. Washington, DC: Island Press, 1996.

Feshbach, Murray and Alfred Friendly. *Ecocide in the USSR*. New York, NY: Basic Books, 1992.

Freeman, A. Myrick and Raymond J. Kopp. "Assessing Damages from the Valdez Oil Spill." *Resources for the Future* (Summer 1989): 5–7.

Freese, Curtis H. *Wild Species as Commodities*. Washington, DC: Island Press, 1998.

Friedman, Mitch. "Earth in the Balance Sheet." *Wild Earth* (Spring 1998), 60–65.

Fullerton, Don and Thomas C. Kinnaman. Household's Responses to Pricing Garbage by the Bag. *American Economic Review*, Sept., pp. 971–984, 1996.

Gibbons, Whit. "Why do bootleggers make good conservationists?" http://www.uga.edu/srelherp/ecoview/Eco4.htm. December 7, 1998.

Gore, Al. *Earth in the Balance: Ecology and the Human Spirit*. Boston: Houghton Mifflin Company, 1992.

Grossman, Gene and Paul Krueger. "Economic Growth and the Environment," *Quarterly Journal of Economics*. 110(2): 1995: 353–377.

Hardin, Garret. "The Tragedy of the Commons," *Science* 162 (December 13, 1968).

Hartwick, John and Nancy Olewiler. *The Economics of Natural Resource Use*. New York, NY: Addison-Wesley, 1998.

Heal, Geoffrey. *Nature and the Marketplace*. Washington, DC: Island Press, 2000.

Heilbroner, Robert. *The Making of Economic Society*, 9th edition. New Jersey: Prentice Hall, 1993.

Henisch, Heinz. *The Photographic Experience*. State College, PA: Penn State University Press, 1994.

Kahn, James. *Economic Approach to Environmental and Natural Resources*. New York, NY: The Dryden Press, 1998

Kaufman, Wallace. *No Turning Back*. New York: HarperCollins, 1994.

Kellert, Steven. *The Value of Life: Biological Diversity and Human Society*. Washington, DC: Island Press, 1996.

Kravetz, Stacy. Dry Cleaner's New Wrinkle: Going Green. *Wall Street Journal*, September 3, 1998: p. B1.

Krutilla, John. "Conservation Reconsidered." *American Economic Review* v. 57, 1967: 777–786.

Lehr, Jay and Carol Bast, "Kyoto is Dead." *Environment and Climate News*, The Heartland Institute, vol. 4, no. 5, May 2001, pp. 1, 13–14.

Leopold, Aldo. *A Sand County Almanac*. New York, NY: Ballantine Books, 1970.

Lindler, Bert. "Making Economics Less Dismal." *High Country News* (October 10), 10, 1988.

Lopez, Barry. *Rediscovery of North America*. New York: Random House. 1992.

Martin, William, Helen Ingram, Nancy Laney, and Adrian Griffin. *Saving Water in A Desert City*. Washington, DC: Resources for the Future, 1984.

Meiners, Roger and Bruce Yandle. *The Common Law: How it Protects the Environment*. Bozeman, MT: PERC, Issue Number PS-13, May 1998.

Milbrath, Lester. *Learning to Think Environmentally: While There is Still Time*. Albany: State University of New York Press, 1996.

Mitchell, John G. "In the Wake of the Spill." *National Geographic* March 1999, v. 195, no. 3, pp. 96–117.

Mundell, Robert. *Man and Economics*. New York, NY: McGraw-Hill, 1968.

National Wildlife Foundation. "Higher Ground," 1997.

Nordhaus, William. *Managing the Global Commons*. MIT Press, 1994.

Nordhaus, William, ed., *Economics and Policy Issues in Climate Change*. Washington, DC: Resources for the Future, 1998.

Norton, Seth. "Property Rights, the Environment, and Economic Well-Being," in *Who Owns the Environment*, edited by Peter Hill and Roger Meiners, Rowman & Littlefield, 1998.

Oates, Wallace, ed. *The RFF Reader in Environmental and Resource Management*. Resources for the Future: Washington, 1999.

O'toole, Randall. *Fixing the Endangered Species Act*. www.teleport.com/~rot/esa.html, 1995.

Orr, David. *Earth in Mind*. Washington, DC: Island Press, 1994.

Portney, Paul. "Counting the Cost," *Environment* March 1998: 14–18, 36–38.

Pompe, Jeffrey and Travis Knowles, The Safe Harbor Program for Red-Cockaded Woodpeckers in South Carolina. Unpublished manuscript. Francis Marion University, Florence, SC, 2001.

Postel, Sandra. "Increasing Water Efficiency." In *State of the World 1986*. New York, NY: W. W. Norton, 1986.

Rathje, William L. *Rubbish*. New York, NY: HarperCollins, 1992.

Repetto, Robert. "Nature's Resources As Productive Assets." *Challenge* 32 (Sept/Oct. 1989), 16–20.

Richards, Bill. "Fishermen in Alaska." *Wall Street Journal*, 9-4-96, p. 1.

Rifkin, Jeremy. *The Biotech Century*. New York: Tarcher/Putnam, 1998.

Rinehart, James and Jeffrey Pompe. "Entrepreneurship and Coastal Resources Management." *Independent Review*, 1, 4, Spring 1997:543–559.

Rinehart, James and Jeffrey Pompe. "The Lucas Case and the Conflict over Property Rights." In *Land Rights: The 1990s Property Rights Rebellion*, edited by Bruce Yandle. Lanham, MD: Rowman and Littlefield, 1995, pp. 67–101.

Rinehart, James and Jackson F. Lee. "The Optimum Level of Ignorance: Marginal Analysis in Education." *The Education Forum* v. 52, 2, Winter 1988, 24–28.

Roodman, David. *Natural Wealth of Nations: Harnessing the Market for the Environment*. New York: W. W. Norton, 1998.

Rubin, Jonathan, Gloria Helfand, and John Loomis. "A Benefit-Cost Analysis of the Northern Spotted Owl." *Journal of Forestry Research* 89, 1991:25–30.

Ryback, Timothy. "The Dutch Dilemma: Is It Art? Is It Trash? Or Is It Both?" *ARTnews*, Nov. 1997, pp. 210–214.

Schiller, Erin. "Delhi Fly and Property Rights can Coexist." *LA Times*, June 19, 1998.

Sedjo, Roger. "The Global Environmental Effects of Local Logging Cutbacks." *Resources* no. 117, Fall 1994, pp. 777–786.

Simmons, Randy. "Fixing the Endangered Species Act," in *Envirocapitalism*, pp. 83–113, 1997.

Simpson, R. David, Roger Sedjo, and John W. Reid. "Valuing Biodiversity for Use in Pharmaceutical Research." *Journal of Political Economy* 104, 1996: 163–185.

Solomen, Caleb. "What Really Pollutes? Study of Refinery Proves an Eye-Opener." *Wall Street Journal*, March 29, 1993, p. 1.

Soule, Michael. "Biophilia: Unanswered Questions." In S. R. Kellert and E. O. Wilson, eds. *The Biophilia Hypothesis*. Washington, D.C.: Island Press, pp. 441–455, 1993.

Sowell, Thomas. "Disaster Aid," *Post and Courier Newspaper*, Charleston, SC, April 4, 1998, p. 11a.

The State. "Environmentalists Sue Forestry Service, Claiming Logging Not Profitable." Dec. 18, 1998, p. a25.

The State. "Norwegian City Tries Feeways to Reduce Congestion, Pollution" Aug. 23, 1998, p. a8.

Taylor, Jeffrey. "New Rules Harness Power of Free Markets to Curb Air Pollution." *Wall Street Journal*, April 14, 1992, p. 1.

Tietenberg, Tom. *Environmental and Natural Resource Economics*. New York, NY: HarperCollins, 1996.

Turner, R. Kerry, David Pearce, and Ian Bateman. *Environmental Economics*. Baltimore: Johns Hopkins Univ., 1993.

United Nations. *Human Development Report*. Oxford University Press, Inc., New York, NY, 1998.

Waldman, Peter. "Desperate Indonesians Devour Country's Trove of Endangered Species." *Wall Street Journal*. October 26, 1998, p. 1.

Welch, Lee Ann. "Property Rights Conflicts Under the Endangered Species Act: Protection of the Red-Cockaded Woodpecker." In *Land Rights: The 1990s' Property Rights Rebellion*, edited by Bruce Yandle. Lanham, MD: Rowman and Littlefield, 1995, pp. 151–198.

Williams, Walter. *All It Takes is Guts*. New York, NY: Regenery Books, 1987.

Wilson, Edward O. *Consilience: The Unity of Knowledge*. New York: Alfred A. Knopf, 1998.

———. *On Human Nature*. Cambridge, MA: Harvard Univ. Press, 1978.

Yandle, Bruce. *Bootleggers, Baptists, and Global Warming*. Bozeman, MT: Political Economy Research Center, 1998.

Index